T0063276

Poems, Two

ROY SHIFRIN

POEMS, TWO

Copyright © 2014 Roy Shifrin.

All rights reserved. No part of this book may be used or reproduced by any means, graphic, electronic, or mechanical, including photocopying, recording, taping or by any information storage retrieval system without the written permission of the publisher except in the case of brief quotations embodied in critical articles and reviews.

Cover: Dancing Death, bronze 14 inches

iUniverse books may be ordered through booksellers or by contacting:

iUniverse
1663 Liberty Drive
Bloomington, IN 47403
www.iuniverse.com
1-800-Authors (1-800-288-4677)

Because of the dynamic nature of the Internet, any web addresses or links contained in this book may have changed since publication and may no longer be valid. The views expressed in this work are solely those of the author and do not necessarily reflect the views of the publisher, and the publisher hereby disclaims any responsibility for them.

Any people depicted in stock imagery provided by Thinkstock are models, and such images are being used for illustrative purposes only. Certain stock imagery © Thinkstock.

ISBN: 978-1-4917-5711-6 (sc)
ISBN: 978-1-4917-5712-3 (e)

Library of Congress Control Number: 2014922801

Printed in the United States of America.

iUniverse rev. date: 01/08/2015

Illustrations

All art works by author

CITY MORGUE

Death's minion came
No, not a gentleman neat in tie and dark suit
Or a winged angel in bright robes
Or softly as on a scented breeze
Or gently with a lover's touch

Death's minion came
In a stained white apron laughing, hands in dirty
        rubber gloves
Smelling of detachment and disinfectant out from a
        noisy hall
Unzipping the large shiny black plastic bag
The industrial shroud of unsentimental disposal

Death's minion came
Into this the last place for the lately lost and left
To he who perhaps once felt himself the center
        of worlds
A driver of great wheels,
That muscled arm falling out from the black plastic
        (seen but for a moment) now thin and
        withered, just before a zipper's fearful
        final sound

Death's minion came
To him maybe long ago noted in song and fable
A fallen hero here upon this steel well-polished slab
Stripped and repackaged for the icy vault, a
        numbered door, the dark

1

Awaiting only papers to be signed, releasing to next
      of kin, if any or if not — better not to know

Death's minion came
With a job to do
Be it called corpse or cadaver
To quickly prepare it for delivery to eternity — some
      he, she, I, or you, someone death, but not his
      minion knew.

BRUEGEL'S ICARUS

They may have heard a cry but they did not look up
A distant shout of "father", or "help", as if a child's cry
The sound of wind through crumpling wings, the breaking
        of wooden struts
A smell of melting wax on the breeze
Then a splash far off, easily mistaken for gentle waves
        upon the shore
Or off the prow of that passing ship

Most likely they did hear it, but felt it didn't concern them.
A plowman must keep his eyes on the plow
Fixed on keeping the upturning rows straight before him
His thoughts on the young seedlings, of harvesting a ripe crop,
        the down to earth necessities of feeding his family
And the young shepherd with his flock staring off as if in a
        dream?
There among the sounds of bleating perhaps thinking that

someday he may leave that flock, put down his staff
be a poet, write meaningful poems if only inspiration,
something novel and new, might happen out here
on this lonely mountainside

But no, nothing new ever happens here just labor and a
        passing dream
Above them the sun shines, clouds pass foretelling of rain
        or shine
And below a ship in full-sail voyages by, as another so
        ordinary day passes

FALLEN POETS

The poets, Wilfred Owen, Rupert Brooke, Isaac Rosenberg,
      A.G. West, Alan Seeger, Charles Sorley
Died in the trenches during World War One.
Their works were little known when that shot, literally
      or not, pierced their hearts.
Might they have survived, as did their poems, had they
      worn them, page after penciled page, bound tight
      about their chests?
So many lines, angry, sad lines, longing, love and love of life,
Could they have stopped that fatal shot, literally or not?
Can poems save lives in times of war?
Are all poets, all the arts, bound to be in the front lines,
      hearts exposed to shot, literally or not?

THERE MAY BE A GOD

There may be a god
But whatever name we give it, this god knows no religion
Not a thought or concern for holy pomp, piety or potentates,
Gold encrusted crowns, miters, sacred books, vast temples.
Not a thought for afterlives, heavens, hells, nirvanas
Good or bad, the blessed or beastly poor, meek or cruel,
       devout or hardened heretics, the unrepentant
       nonbelievers
Not a thought or concern for sky and clouds
Great seas, vast lands, grasses, shrubs, or trees
Nothing for birds, fish, the multitude of beasts, or
       some self-centered higher primates

This god is a god beyond all awe and wonder
An existence manifest in the vastness of time and space
Of infinites, where stars, galaxies, dark and light energy
       churn and tumble in configurations and patterns
       of muons, leptons, pions, and on and ons
Born back in some pin point where matter itself first mattered
       and all movement began
Back in a fiery furnace when time first ticked predicting a distant
       future as a cold hushed death in the stillness of the last
       vibrating atom and then absolute nothing forever
Such a god self logging-in in a length and breath numberless to
       measure, only as anomalies and singularities

And we? We, those self centered higher primates laughingly
       calling ourselves much loved by such a god

Arrogantly making so much of our existence, our future, our past,
      progress, profit, and posterities
We, but evolution's roll of the dice surviving precariously on a
      speck of slag spun off into an insignificant corner of causality.
Rarely asking ourselves what could we really mean to a god,
      fearful of the sad answer - nothing, nothing absolutely
      nothing.

There may be a god, but in our nothingness, absolute nothingness it
      is we and we alone who have to invent meaning for our
      existence
Clinging to a vain hope, prayer, faith, that what we do here, there,
      now, and then, may some day be something that such a god
      made in our imaginings might notice.

OF MY LOVE

What flowers can I send
That of my love you'll know?

What words can I write
That as love poems you'll read them so?

What songs can I sing?
That my love will ring out clear?

What embrace can I give
That of my love you'll feel it near?

Tell me any other acts of love that I might do
That you, so doubtful, will believe it true?

THE MEEK AND MILD

We the meek and mild lining up in rows one behind the other
Far from the open fields we've left behind where grass grew
     abundant and we grazed without limits.
We are the cows of many colors, the sheep of varied fleece.
Now together marching down barred tracks and gated paths
     to stand before this metal door.
From inside strange sounds of mechanical wheels and horrible
     cries as if of cleaving knives and whirring saws cutting flesh.

Why are we here?
What awaits us is clearly beyond our simple comprehension.
We who have been so well behaved and docile, have lived our lives
     following obediently the shepherd's crook.
True, there are terrible tales the horses tell of the misbehaved and
     rebellious sent to suffer the opening of flesh, peeling of skin,
     emptying of organs still warm on to a saw-dusted floor
     running in blood and gore.
Then so quickly up and hung upside down on hooks,

onto cables that will carry them
To be sliced into steaks and chops transformed from living flesh
        into meat
Wrapped, packaged in plastic, to be stacked on
        refrigerated shelves.
So unbelievable, and what do draft horses know?
Surely we who wait here, images of our loving master, are of more
        significance than but to bringing dietary pleasures and profit
        to strangers far from these fields.
No, best calmly accept that such foreboding sounds are far
        beyond our comprehension.

So when the doors open let us enter proudly with heads held high.
We are the cows and sheep long obedient to the shepherd's wave
        and whistle
The meek and mild who have been told that beyond these doors
        are fields of such lushness, more than our simple natures
        could ever comprehend, a promised place where we shall
        surely all graze in peace forever.

IF I RECITED

I said, "What if I recited love poems that you'd call
So well crafted they conquered your heart, soul, and all
Aflaming desires so bright that this very night
Into bed with this poet you'd fall"

She answered, "Instead, what if I gave you a critique full and fair
A parsing of your poems both insightful and rare
So impressed you would be that surely we'd see
If in these lines one might find some true talent there"

I said, "The best critique is if my words can beguile
Some lovely lips into a compliant smile
For art's sake your charms swift into my arms
For poetic passion with meter and style"

She answered, "I must confess your rhymes sometimes sing
But poetry and seduction is not the same thing
I prefer the poetic phrase that endures beyond a few days
And not written for some sexual success it may bring"

Dear reader, you will understand this poem I trust,
Is a dialogue between poet and muse not just one of lust.

MATTER

With a chisel, a hammer, perhaps an ax
God split the void into two perfect halves
What was inside was whipped to batter
Knowing it to be the stuff of matter

Matter it is, yes or no, no matter
For it is all mathematics to you and me
Scientists say the universe we know
Is best understood when baked as dough

Such dough, needed, and by God so kneaded
Out from his stellar oven arose all we need to know
Yet we, mostly ignorant of these facts they tell,
Best believe from a better batter a better
        mankind will arise as well

JUSTICE AS ON COURT TV

Jack killed Ed in a fit of rage
Ed's wife with Bill had a tryst
But Bill put his arm in a lion's cage
And lost his hand to the wrist

Jack, the lion's owner, felt no blame
Pleading of right and wrong beasts have scant breath
Ed's wife brought a lawsuit all the same
Demanding Jack and the lion be put to death

H. H. Harold, the judge, heard the case
With Bill's mangled hand on show
Ruling that ignorance for the lion had no place
Since not to eat hands even beasts should know

Ed, through a medium, gave evidence though dead
Said his wife urged Jack to do him in
And backed up every word the lion said

Insisting murder compared to mangling was
      the greater sin

"Guilty," pronounced judge Harold, the justly famed,
Condemning Jack and the lion with their lives to pay
Ed's wife for adultery jailed while Bill was caned
For not knowing from hand-eating lions to stay away

TIME BACK THEN

Can I ever again think of time
As I thought of time back then
Days as everything moved as they would go
And all that wasn't now was surely only when

I rose when everyday was brand new
To be spent wisely foolishly without a thought
Minutes, hours, days, weeks them all
As if riches I hadn't bought

My mirrored face remained unchanged
Every morning as in bed it was put away
The body grew bigger stronger without effort
All tomorrows so simple proving forever was nature's way

YOU ARE BEAUTIFUL

You are beautiful.
Right now so beautiful.
You show me a picture of when you were young
Tall and thin, long light brown hair, fair smooth skin,
Smiling for the camera or perhaps for him
      who held the camera
But you are now not happy.
You tell me that you must lose ten pounds.
That your hair is too short and there are traces of gray.
Saying, see what gravity has done to your breasts, arms, thighs
There are now small wrinkles around your eyes
You would never dare wear those tight jeans now
Nor dare smile before a camera knowing what it would show,
      the truth you say.
It is twenty years later and you are not the same.
Yet, in my twenty-year-older eyes you are even more beautiful
It's not flattery but true

What you see as imperfections is what I love
Those years written on our bodies have been well spent.
Together time's beauty will be ours forever, youth's beauty
       is only lent.

FACING DEATH

I am determined not to bend or bow
To plead crying out in fear, nor whine
When you come to tie and knot
That toe-tag marking my apparent end with time

Know, that I intend to face you eye to eye
Acting bravely should you say I've passed away
Waving some official papers denoting name,
      and date, this place and time of day

You may even try to drape a sheet over my head
While whispering "good-bye" in my ear
And sanctimoniously telling me to rest in peace
No, off with that sheet, I'll refuse to hear

Yes, I know that so far you have always won
So far no one has refused your call

These tombstones your trophies go on and on
But at graveside I intend to still stand tall

I plan to refuse to go gently to my rest
Never giving in to that forever night
Death may well be inevitable, even logical
But life's irrational; I will not go without a fight

GOD MADE MAN

In his image God made man
A clever concept but faulty plan

For he who made the sea and sky
Didn't plan ahead or wonder why

Having a macho-man to rule his earth
Devoid of wisdom to judge its worth?

From loin-clothed plunderer now in a suit
Destroyer of Edens from branch to root

Clearly even a God could seriously err
Or done it better if He were a Her

A FOND FAREWELL

Let me wish you a fond farewell as here you read
For it appears we as the whole human species has a fatal flaw
A chromosomal misalignment that drives us to destroy our
   habitat for greed
Not for food, water, more sex, song, surely not only enough
   to live but to have ever more

In that mossy glen where we and all life together did and do thrive
By adapting to this world, evolving by Darwin's game both for the
   eater and the eaten
The wiser or bigger, or by just sharper teeth to remain alive
But man soon changed the rules by inventing gods who justified
   him as the master of this Eden

There are many Darwinian reasons Trilobites to Dinosaurs over
   the eras died
Yet ignorant humans with their invented gods call it holy,
   if necessary to destroy the planet earth
With sweet sounding words of love, peace, benevolence as another
   ancient predator with speech thy lied
Invented individual wealth as the more valuable then that which
   gives this world and life its worth

LAND OF GREED

Living in this land of greed
The perfect place for those as rich as we
Where I have mine, more than I need
And the dream that what is yours, will
        someday belong to me

No false modesty here, no sense of moral obligation
With our growing wealth ostentatiously on display
Exhibiting that inequality is the basis of this nation
Where the poor are taxed believing it patriotic for
        them to pay our way

Religion, that loyal dog, following where power's bound
Preaching that such vast excesses are not a sin
For the docile poor vast riches will be in heaven found
As the Holy Books teach and actually believed, thank God,
        as it has always been

In this land of greed each must contentedly know their place
The rich to plunder, the plundered nose to grindstone earn
Insuring today the moneyed few live as a Master Race
And tomorrow? – the far tomorrow?
        That's not of greed's concern

LOVE SONG

A fresh flowering of passion spreading swiftly as Poison Ivy
Words as Jays squabbling over a squirrel's carcass
Embraces but the foretelling of a coming frostbite
Lips hiding rows of K-9s ready to bite or better chew

All that, once forgotten, returns anew
That vivid lie of love between us two

Life together as tethered toiling in a salt mine no days off
Nights of fearful dreams of tomorrow's awakening
Each morning rewinding a watch that tells no time
Promises of another new day with nothing new

Well noted now what I always knew
Memories of the pain that once was you

Resentments fertile as fields where willows weep
Daily pinpricks to an already punished heart

Bones bent and broken as a cracked cane to carry on
All this and more, saying, we don't mind, not us two

Suffering in silent as silent sufferers do
All this is how I remember you

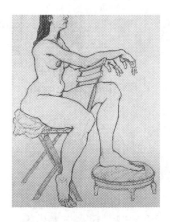

TO HER OF THE SOUTHWORLD

I, pale and shy dream of floating up from a deep Mediterranean on
    to beaches where orange orchards sweet-scent the air
Where words of love, wet, warm, and sun-filled flow all tingling
    with vowel endings light and lilting on the tongue.
But no, not from me, for I am of northern stock and worlds, my
    words, sweet, free, and warm freeze in the rising from
    heart to lips.
Harsh and hoarse I sound— you turn away

You a rainbow in my eyes colorful as the birds of tropical climes
Those that sing as the nightingale, the canary, and the thrush,
    or softly as the dove from a dark-leafed bower
Songs I would wish to answer as such jungle lovers seek their mates
But I can sing only the song of the snow goose, the stormy petrel,
    the lonely cry of the herring gull

From me comes the North wind's caws and croaks — you
 	hold your ears

In my heart a string orchestra plays concertos in a plaza of palm
 	trees and bubbling fountains
With choruses of violins, cellos, bass and harps, vibrating as one
 	to my desire
I, their conductor, baton held high, wave them on and up from
 	below your open window
Such beauty that you have never heard before and in hearing will
 	know the true me
But fearful of rejection, timid, so reserved of manner and gesture,
 	my music drowns in the roar of snowplows and blowers —
 	your window closes

So from my land of wind and snow, blizzard and flake, in
 	desperation I send to you these written words. Please read
 	them and know — know that for love of you even this
 	frostbitten fearful heart can hot with passion flow.

SHE WHO SO WANTED TO PLEASE

She who so wanted to please

Not pleasure for herself, but me
Those afternoons, the cold basement studio, our bed
      the concrete floor, her fear of roaches.
We placed newspapers down but her
      eyes, beautiful eyes, looked
      nervously about.
She undressed, I undressed, our clothing
      hung on an old paint stained easel.

She who so wanted to please.

We lay upon the cold newspaper in the
      light of bare florescent bulbs

The radio in the corner tuned to music
           was now news, death, war, a
           killing uptown.
Above outside the sound of rushing feet,
           cars honking, buses, our eyes went
           to the one window.
The shade was not all the way down.
She thought, I thought, could we be seen?
We made love.

She who so wanted to please.

It was over. She smiled relieved.
Relieved, now we could stand up.
No further fear of roaches, our bodies off
           the cold paper covered concrete.
We could pull the shade all the way down,
           get dressed, leave this so cold place
Perhaps to a coffee house to hold hands,
           to be romantic, that would please her.

While we dressed her soft hand caressed
           my cheek
As if to check, to see if I was satisfied.
I smile, she smiles.

She who so wanted to please
To please a so selfish young artist.

THE COUPLE

I saw them as I wrote poetry in the library
My mind wandering as it often does
She a beauty, full of life and joy
While he oblivious to just how wonderful she was

Matted hair, torn shirt, what was he even doing here?
No reader he more the image of the pillaging Hun
While she in a thin summer dress brightly danced
        among the storied stacks
Making those book-bound heroines jealous of her, a
        glowing sun

Around him she put her arms to give a kiss
As he coldly pushed her away. I could see
It was pearls offered to a swinish man
And thought, what a waste, better place that
        kiss on me

"Come" she whispered, inviting him into a darkened bay
There I was sure to offer him her perfect breast
He ignoring walked head-down towards the door
As I imagined the pleasure of it caressed

They left and left me sitting with these ragged lines
Thinking of beauty and wondering why
She so perfect was wasting time with him
While here sat a poet, a lover — none more
        appreciative of her than I

THE VISIT

She sat in a chair on the green lawn
In the shade of a tree as we sat around her.
Just a shadow bent forward staring down at her
      hands never looking up.
In Public School I remember being jealous when her
      teacher told the class how brilliant she was,
      an IQ near 200 or higher.
"How did she like it here?" we asked.
"It's fine," she said without emotion, twisting
      a lock of her hair.
At thirteen so far above her fellow students she was
      given a scholarship and went off to study
      science at university.
"What do you do during the day?" we asked.
"I sew. I am working on an apron with bears on it."
I remember standing with the adults as she was
      the center of attention.

She was explaining to them some recently discovered
        flaws in Einstein's Theory Of Relativity.
"And the food, how is the food?" we asked.
She smiled slightly, apparently assuming we thought
        institutional food a joke.
"It's OK," she said as she smoothed a crease in her skirt.
We sat for a long time in silence, birds sang, and
        a warm breeze blew.
A kind man came over to tell us it was time
        for her to return to her room.
We all rose. Her sister gave her a kiss as the kind man
        led her towards the austere gray building
"Our mother was so proud," her sister said,
"Everyone called her so gifted, so special, so much
        smarter than all her playmates, certainly
        destined for great things."
The door of the austere gray building closed
"And all she ever wanted to be was ordinary."

THIS FIELD

In a New Hampshire field with Maples aligned in a long
     majestic band
There I saw the poet Robert Frost seated with his pad and
     pen in hand

Today it's all backhoes, chain saws, condominiums where once
     wild nature was before
I shout to a workmen, "Is the poet Frost about?" The answer, "you
     mean that old guy who sat about and wrote? – No. No more.

CRUEL DEATH VISITS EMILY DICKENSON

"Come with me," death said,
"Leave your pen and ink behind,
Poetry's hard – this world's unkind,
It's a fool's path that you tread."

"Ask yourself, why
Of poets and poetry who'll care?
Posterity will not spare
Your scribblings, they too with you shall die"

She answered, "No, it's by but words I live.
I've been alone all of my life
Neither mother nor a wife
Just these poems the world I give."

"Page after page I fill
Of days lived just for art
Words noting every part
Of life's story, wish, and will."

Death sneered, "Beyond this tiny room
No one cares you see,
All just wasted labor – and your destiny?
To be forgotten in the tomb."

HOMAGE TO W H AUDEN

W H Auden I greatly fear
Would be unhappy returning here
Finding well-crafted poetry has fled
Ignored by the public, and so seldom read

Now free verse, prose poems abound
Hardly poetry mostly sound
Depth and passion are things long lost
Along with style and wit also so tossed

For today anything is called a poem
Anywhere keypad or pen may roam
Mark it down have no shame
Nothing's serious, it's all just a game

Contemporary poetry is not an art
Where skill and depth play any part

Just avoid rhythm especially rhyme
Words that sing in step while marking time

Or that which moves the soul when heard
Or proudly boasts the profound word
So to master Auden, a reverential bow
He, and poetry, share the same place now

GREEN WHEELBARROW

(a case for Dr. W C Williams)

Who realized so much would depend on that red wheelbarrow
      after we painted it green?
You left it in that wooded glen and now it can't be seen
It's surely there, dear, for why else would those pigeons
      strut about, their feathers oh so bright
Unfortunately the sun soon sets and you'll not find the thing
      out there this dark and stormy night
Stubborn, blindly searching, rain glazed your bare baldhead –
      I told you to wear a hat
You caught a cold, pneumonia, died – and the once red
      wheelbarrow?
That was all there was of that.

WAR

War you have a long history
We inherited you with sharp teeth and claws
We named you necessary and natural
Prosperity through conquest
Servant to the cross, crescent, and despot
Glorified in song and story
Creator of bronze heroes in plazas
Generous patron of wheelchairs and crutches
Planter of the honored dead
Harvester of pain and loss
Hypocrite during reverential moments of silence
Forever waged in the name of right
Or somehow waged in the name of peace
We may have inherited you with sharp teeth and
      claw
But by evolution we have succeeded in making you
      so much more

BASIC TRAINING

I looked in the mirror and saw a young killer
There I was again in fatigues, in my helmet, my
      rifle held before me
Ahead the first signs of dawn, a long road, a mess hall
      at its end
A place where we would stack rifles, hang up helmets,
      rest and if able, eat
In a wider mirror I saw us all, packed tightly together running,
      sweating, breathing heavily
Each trying to stay in step

"One, two, three, four, one, two, three, four", the sergeant
      leading us shouted
Spending precious breath we repeated, "one, two, three, four,
      one, two, three, four"
"What are you?" the sergeant shouted without pause for breath
Trained every morning in this routine we knew the answer,
"We're killers"

"Louder, I can't hear you"
We shouted, "We're killers"
"And what do you like to do?"
We answered, "To kill"
"Louder, I can't hear you"
We shouted, "To kill"
"Then let's hear you growl like killers" the sergeant demanded
We growled imagining how killers might growl
"Louder, I can't hear you"
We growled the louder

Beside me the tough and timid, the fearless and fearful,
      together counting steps all wondering what the
      future held while parroting we liked to kill
The sun rose, the perspiration ran down our faces, and again the call,
"One, two, three, four, one, two, three, four."
In that old mirror, such young faces not knowing what lay ahead,
      that familiar path, or a foreign war

THE WALL

We brought him over and stood him before the wall
He was an old man, burnt brown, wrinkled face, his clothes just rags
So foreign, so different, clearly not understanding why he was there
        or a word of our language.

"Shoot him," the sergeant shouted.
The corporal with his weapon didn't move.

The old man looked at us as we leaned against the truck
        or stretched out in the shade of the wall
He seemed to be wondering if this had anything to do with him.

"Shoot him," the sergeant shouted.
The corporal didn't move.

Perhaps the old man thought it was about the bag he was holding.
He raised it up to show us, perhaps to give it to us.
He nodded as if to say, take it, look at it.

"Shoot him," the sergeant shouted
The corporal didn't move

Our eyes went from the sergeant to the corporal. What was
        happening? What had happen? Was it something we
        didn't know about?
We looked at our shouting sergeant and the standing corporal.

"Shoot him, he's the one," the sergeant shouted.
The corporal didn't move.

The old man seemed relieved. The shouting wasn't about
        him.
He seemed sure that it had nothing to do with him.
This was some foreign problem, something concerning strangers.
He took off his hat, slowly bowed as if the custom when bidding
        good-bye, put it back on his head and took a step to go
The corporal shouted, "don't move", and shot him dead.

NATIONAL SOCCER HALL OF FAME

SILHOUETTES

He was walking along as if strolling
A silhouette against the desert sky
I could see, could it be perhaps the form of a rifle hanging from
     his shoulder
In his mouth a cigarette, he puffed and there was a cloud of
     smoke about his head
Though he was far off I was sure that I could hear singing
Was he singing to himself? Was here a happy man?
He stopped, I tensed, but it was only to watch the silhouette
     of a bird fly by
He was looking up for so long, perhaps he was a birdwatcher.
Did he have a book at home with pictures of different species?
Would he enthusiastically tell them that he had seen a
     whatever it might be called?
He exhaled cigarette smoke and again started walking.
I could now see sand rising up around his boots as
     he kicked a stone.

He had no idea that I was there, no worry, he seemed
        to have no worries at all
From his breast pocket he took out something
His head bent forward as if he were reading
Was it orders listing, time, place, and objective?
Or perhaps a letter of love from his girl, or of worry
        from his mother
Would they be waiting for him wondering where he was,
        when he would be coming back?
He stopped again. Perhaps he sensed that I was there.
He suddenly looked up. There were no birds to be seen.
Fearful, I fired and he fell. A silhouette very still on the ground
"Just a dumb-F, imagine just walking along out there alone,
        singing, looking at birds" they say, laughing loudly
        when I tell them.
Hardened vets, laughing loudly when I tell them
Too loudly, as ones thinking of their own silhouettes

SOLDIER'S SONG

Think of the coming dawn my love, this promise, and of me
For this very night I'm bound for war
Across a vast and troubled sea

Think well my love, of your moon and stars brightly up above
Though the flash of battle lights my night
Only death will ever end my love

Think best upon the tide, my love, its ebb and daily turning
Though battles as the sea may rage
I dream the ebb, and on the tide to you returning

WE HERE

Let me wish you a fond farewell as here you read that
We, as the whole human species, posses a fatal flaw
A chromosomal misalignment that drives us to destroy our own
        habitat
Not just gathering food, water, sex, song, surely not for just
        necessities to live but to have ever and ever more

In that mossy glen where all nature once did thrive
By adapting to its habitat, evolving slowly each through great
Darwin's game both the eaters and the eaten
The wiser or bigger, by sharper tooth or stronger jaw evolved
        to remaining alive
Not so man – this recent arrival soon changed the game by
        inventing Gods that gave him right to rule over this Eden

There are reasons Trilobites to Dinosaurs over eons
        each have died away
While we recent arrivals cleverly wrote new rules that gave
        us all of planet earth
In these books with sweet sounding words of love, peace, benevolence
        we perpetuate such a lie
So that our selfish gains will be the new Darwin game where all
        life not serving man will die

THE BUTCHER'S WINDOW

On a London street, in a butcher's window
A great mosaic of chops, ribs, livers and heart
With crushed ice, parsley, and bright white tags
Pricing flesh and bone as if works of art.

An art more beautiful than living lambs, cow or pigs
Freely frolicking in field or sty
Proof that the only reason they exist
Is in parts that whet the appetite, beguile the eye

Beyond this glass death could not better be displayed
Sculpted by the cleaver's cuts and hacking saw
Nature's innocent slaughtered for our sake
Butchery, without all its blood and gore

MYSTERY

I stopped the car
Before me lay a great field of snow
Snow untouched, white to the horizon
Even whiter against the gray late afternoon sky
Bright to a far filigree of bare black trees
I would take a picture of such barren beauty
Stepping out into the cold I raised my camera
But the field of snow was not untouched, not barren
Before me from the road lay a line of foot prints
Foot prints, not snowshoes, not skis, someone had
      recently walked the knee-deep snow to the
      horizon, to the distant dark line of trees
Mystery replaced photography
There was no house for miles. Who had walked this
      field? Where was he or she going?
There was no track of a faithful dog running
      beside this traveler

No hoof marks of a deer that a hunter might
        be stalking
I waited beside the beautiful empty field
Would the walker return, had they fallen
        or gotten lost in that far wood?
Should I follow, should I go for help?
It was far too cold to be outside, outside at night,
        outside and alone
As I stood it grew dark
Too dark for a picture
I hesitated, but shivering I returned to my car
        and drove off.

THE WAY

"This is the way to go," he said

I follow

"This is the way to go, down these stairs where the way is steep"

I follow

"This is the way to go where the way is steep, the path
      so very dark"

I follow

"This is the way, steep and dark, and without knowing
      what you shall find ahead"

I follow

"This way ever so uncertain, the goal remote, where there
      may be great danger"

I follow

"May I ask why" he said, "Why do you follow? What do you
      hope to find?

I follow hoping to find that this is the way, so steep and dark,
      unknown, remote, dangerous, all uncertain, but most
      of all, that this is the only way to find what is worth finding

LESS REAL

It seems so long ago
That night, the street I always walked
He stepped out of the doorway
"Give me your money"
The gun, was it real or a toy
Was this a joke, I looked at the gun
"Quick, give me your money"

What to do, what should I do?
I could laugh as if he were joking
I could yell in the hope of scaring
   him to run away
I could run believing he would not
   really shoot me
I could grab the gun, as in the movies
Wrestle it from his hand, throw him
   to the ground
"Hands up" I would say and lead him
   to a Police Station
Turn him in
"How brave" the police officers would say

"Give me all you got and quick"
He looked at me, waving the gun
I looked at him as he waved the gun
And then it happened as if in
   an instant

That instant
My hand, the shot, the flash, the blood
Did it really happen or am I disguising it
        as a poem
To make it seem less real
To heal that scar from so
        long ago

MEN IN SUITS

They came to the door
Two men in suits
From their ears
From the plugs in their left ears
Ran coiled wires
Disappearing inside their suit jackets

"Is your father here?" one asked unsmiling
"Why" I replied
"Is your father here?" he asked again
"Who are you?" I replied
"Is your father here?" he asked
As if he could speak no other words
"Why do you want my father?" I replied
"Is your father here?" he asked
Then his left eye, the one near the ear
        plug rose
As if he were listening to an order
They looked at one another
Then turned and walked down the hallway
        and were gone

They never did return, never
But my parents from then on lived expecting
        they'd be back
I don't know why, or why
My father always had his suitcase packed

TO THINK THOUGHTS

I thought thoughts
And in thinking them thought that
    I had made a thing.

Does not thoughts equal things?

This thought surely was more
    than just a thought.
A thought turned into that thing, made
    from nothing, yet more than just
    thoughts of things.
So thinking of things made of thoughts,
    thinking thoughts and through such
    thoughts thinking of things.

    I thought

And thinking that thoughts equal things
    soon a thing did appear.
And it was true, for is not this thought
    a poem right here?

IF AND LOVE

If you will love
Knowing in love that there may be pain
Or that love, knowingly or unknowingly, may
      cruelly pass you by

And if in your very being
You know that in love there is often little logic
Its actions, only befuddled answers perhaps to
      never know why

You were once beguiled by it's grandeur
Of love existent beyond but mate and marriage
Risking all for reward that makes it all worth
      the try

True life is short, they say
And love even shorter, perhaps for a moment
So that in the end it, you, love, and all shall die

Remember from the beginning you were not born
        with wings
Just desires often the irrational
Believing only by love we best can fly

THE SAME

We met by accident in the park
She was as beautiful as I remembered her
That same smile as she put out her
      hand asking how I was.
So long apart, so long since we had seen
      one another
She looked the same but who was she?

"Do you now live near here or still at the old place?"
      she asked.
"I'm still at the old place, it looks the same,
      do you ever think about it?"
"I remember our buying the furniture," she said,
      "the rug, lamp, table, (a pause) the bed."
"Are they all still there?"
"The same," I said, "just as when you left."

"And her," she asked, "what's her name, the artist
            who's work you so much admired?
Do you still see her, is she living with you?"
"No, as ever we are just friends, I live alone."
She smiled that same smile, the smile I so well
            remember, her smile of not believing.
Then the anger, no smiles, the yelling,
        I would try to explain, no use.

Today just that smile, the same smile

ARTISTS AT SEA

What are we but as the lamps that always burnt brightly fixed
        to this ever tossing ship.
But now these lights shine out in hope of rescue
To be seen on that distant shore, there beyond the roar
        of breakers.
We shout out for help but can they hear?
Would rescue venture out on a night such as this?
"See those distant points of light, the foolish there at sea," those
        on the shore will say. "It was their choice and now they
        must row hard against the cruel current or they are lost."
But we so far from shore, we can no longer row.
Exhausted from years at the oars. Years of believing, believing we
        could keep this ship afloat, dreaming our family on
        a tranquil beach.
Now we hang helpless on the sides

In this rough sea, rough beyond calming, so short a time before
        lamps and all are flooded and will be gone.
But what of those we brought with us in this so small and frail
        a craft? What of them?
We know that we are lost, sinking, soon falling deep beneath
        the waves. But them, what of them, the innocents?
They will have no lamps to guide them, only lifebelts waterlogged
        from so many past storms.
Can they swim without our light, without our arms to hold them
        up? They must. They must now swim alone, swim strongly
        against the pulling swirl of our sinking ship

The lights grow dull, the wave is upon us, and all is dark.
Only the sound of far off breakers on a distant shore as our ship
        slowly turns over and sinks.
The flooded lamps disappear below the waves.
Those on the shore shake their heads and leave for homes on
        higher hills.
Alone in the heartless angry waters only small heads bob.
From below bubbling up from sea filled mouths a cry,
        "Believe."

THE BOTTICELLI SHOW

"What a surprise to meet you here."
No, surprise, she knew it was very likely that we would meet
Why else did she look so beautiful? That tight black dress,
       her face even more beautifully made up, wearing the
       necklace I had given to her so long ago when I said it
       made her look right out of a Botticelli painting ?
"Are you here at the museum to also see the Botticelli show?
Why else would I be here today, she knew how much I
       admired his work.
Smiling she spoke about the artist's life in Italy, she knew so much
       about his art, mentioning the show of his work
       we had seen in Florence
That café after the show where we had lunch, it was to become
       one of our favorite places

Did I remember? She asked.
Of course I remembered.
And the bus trip to Sienna, the pension, it was so hot we

slept out on the terrace?
Questions such questions but the big one we didn't ask
Were we both still alone, unasked, fearful of the answer
          not believing either of us could have possibly
          found anyone else.
No, this meeting was not by chance
I thought, hoped that she might be here.
Beautiful, beautiful, still so beautiful
We paused as if one of us were about to ask that question
We looked at one another waiting, waiting for the other to start but
did not.

We walked through the exhibit trying to make what
          sounded like profound comments
How easy, how natural this had all been in the past
No unasked questions, no trying to sound profound
Memories of later together making love in bed
At the end of the exhibit with the Botticelli exhibit behind us
          we stepped into the hallway

There an awkward pause, a very awkward pause
Were we going to shake hands or exchange kisses on the cheek?
In the end we did neither just said, good-bye and parted
That Botticelli, him of our past would surely have expected more
          from us and was not happy.

FALLING IN LOVE

I fell in love with you even before we met
I knew what you were like, your face, your hair,
        your tenderness
How you would talk, that you would love the things
        I love
Want to do the things that I want to do
Those romantic walks together through the woods
        hand in hand
Our meaningful silences, our shared dreams
And awake at night in each other's arms
All so natural, so soft yet passionate
No "musts", "ought tos", fuss or fumblings
We would be made for each other
It was so easy to fall in love with you even before
        we met

I met you. You did not look as I had imagined
Your face, your hair, you were not soft, tender, or compliant
You had your own dreams and those things that you
        wanted to do
You argued, you hated walking in the woods, hated
        so many things that I loved
You were seldom silent, always full of opinions
We fought in bed, nothing was easy or natural, all "musts"
        "ought tos" and fumblings, but, and the biggest
        but of all,
We could laugh, laugh at each other, laugh together
It was not easy, it was hard, but I fell in love with
        you,

I had it all so wrong and now I know it was so clearly you,
     could only have been you
I would never have fallen in love with you, never,
      until we met

FRIENDS BE JOYOUS
(a la Beethoven)

For it is certain that it shall come
If not tomorrow a soon someday
When mankind shall see itself as one
And know that to be the only way

When poverty will be unknown
Disparity only in gifts of mind and hand
Where wisdom and art are freely sown
And it's harvest the riches of the land

Sing out in joy, sing out, all men are bothers
None called strangers, none called "others"

All shall revere the earth our mother
Old but each spring once more young

As we her children, sisters, bothers
To her bounty our songs are sung

Words "conquered" and "conqueror" shall not exist
With sword, rifle, tank, from the language lost
Peace the potent force none can resist
And warrior's graves but note past history's cost

Sing out in joy, sing out an ode that's never old
When poems and music a better future foretold

Now we seek worlds beyond the sky
Disease and illness all to be cured
In science and technology the answers "why"
And faith and morality through love secured

Look around and see us of now
Are we not a species bred for change
Programmed to learn new ways and how
A better world we can arrange?

So sing out in joy, in joy all sing along
On that quest, we're all bound, and all belong

JAZZ CLUB

No, I'm not here to hear your cry of pain
Don't care to know a tortured soul, or of a life
       lived in a roach infested room
Who cares where you go after hanging up that brilliant
       black tuxedo.
Play, play the tune, make music, smile, show
       me those pearly whites
Make me happy — make it Jazz

No, I'm here to drink, to forget my pain, lost love or money
Don't whine of late nights, hard times, or your
       dreams and hopes
That may be good in church on Sunday but your employed
       here, make me forget, run those black
       fingers across the keys
Make me happy —make it Jazz

No, none of that passion born from slavery past, the lash,
       don't sing of the back of buses, or your father drinking
       from colored only fountains
You're here to perform so just perform, smile, give me a
       syncopated rhyme, have my toe to tap,
       something I can whistle
Make me happy — make it Jazz

No, I really don't see you at all, just something dark and black
       at the piano, or with a trumpet, or a sax
Suck sorrow, suck soul, suck history from that rhythm, show
       off, show how you can twist it free of blackness

Play those up-beat tunes, those boozy blues, improvise,
        make it cool or you don't get paid
Make me happy — make it Jazz

No, so it's not your music, not your heart and soul
Don't think I want to hear you in what you're playing. What
        do I know or care of blackness.
Make music as the ol' slave who smiles to master, doffs his hat on
        passing and say he loves life so
Play me white man's music done in blackface, happy, happy,
        happy, always happy
That makes me happy — make it Jazz

MARSHA AND THE STARRY NIGHT

Marsha plain and shy, teased "sex-starved" by the guys

I hardly knew her we were two young art students far from
      home that hot summer
Unable to sleep, I sat in the rocker on the porch.
Midnight and the street was empty, above the sky sparkled
      a Van Gogh
I dozed, I woke, I dozed, perhaps to dream
Someone called to me from across the silent square lit
      by one street lamp
"Come help me. Can you help me?"
She stood in her nightgown, waving.

It was Marsha plain and shy, teased "sex-starved" by the guys

I rose and crossed the square
She firmly grabbed my hand and led me into her house
"None of the lights work, no lights at all."
She clicked a light switch, "See no lights."
She took my hand leading me upstairs to her bedroom,
      I followed
She pulled the chain on the table lamp beside her bed, "See, no
      lights up here either. When I woke up there were no lights."
In the darkness I was sure I saw her smile.

Smiling Marsha plain and shy, teased "sex-starved" by the guys

I investigated the table lamp, as Marsha stood very close beside me,
      beside her bed
I ran my hand up to the bulb — there was no bulb, the bulb had
      been removed.
Through her bedroom window the sky sparkled even brighter
      with promise
Marsha clearly wanted me. At this midnight witching hour
      empty light sockets were the sure sign of her desire
What to do this star filled night? Dare I ignore seduction? No. That
      would be an insult to her, I reasoned.
We were art students. What about Van Gogh? What about the film,
      "Lust for Life"? What about just plain lust? Wasn't that the
      driving force of art, didn't we all believed that?

So close stood Marsha plain and shy, teased "sex-starved"
      by the guys

I swiftly turned, took Marsha in my arms and kissed her.
Passionate as I thought I was, she pulled away
Struggling in the darkness, locked in each other's arms,
      we fell backwards on to her bed.

It happened in an instant. She let out a scream of terror so loud it
 left a ringing in my ears. We leapt apart ending up on
 opposite sides of the bed.
It had been a joke. Her roommates had come when she was asleep
 and removed all the bulbs.
A prank whose consequences could not have been imagined
 and was soon known to all.

Poor Marsha plain and shy, teased "sex starved" by the guys,
Suffered all the rest of that summer, mocking laughter
 that the taunt had been proven right
And I? I was to become known as "Roy the Rapist" a danger to
 female artists who dared wander out under a Van Gogh's
 starry night.

BLUFF-DADDY

You can't compare Bluff-Daddy to Beethoven
Beethoven is played in fancy concert halls holding
    a few hundred fans
Bluff-Daddy fills a fifty thousand-seat stadium, each ticket sells
    for six or seven hundred dollars or maybe even more,
    if you can even get them
For Beethoven what's it cost, a few hundred dollars at most?
And what a show with Bluff-Daddy when he suddenly leaps
    out on to the stage in his famous red cape and those
    glowing green boots
Cartwheel after cartwheel, explosions everywhere,
    everything hidden by smoke and flames
While strobe lights flash and different colored laser
    beams rake the audience
What is there with Beethoven, men and women in drab
    tuxedos sitting like statues
No one even gets up and smashes his instrument like
    Bluff-Daddy does two or three times
And then there are the "Bluffettes" half-naked dancing girls
    shaking their butts at the audience, then their
    augmented breasts, always the hope that a breast or
    two will fall out
Not at a Beethoven concert, you just sit quiet while nothing
    happens
Bluff-Daddy at least once, maybe more, will grab his crotch
    and the audience goes wild
You never feel alone at a Bluff-Daddy concert, everybody is
    yelling, screaming, the noise of the crowd rings in
    your ears, you feel like you can hardly breath

Does that happen with Beethoven, no, it's as dull and quiet
	as at a funeral
And at the end this guy with a little stick bows and it's all over
You catch a cab or take the subway and go home
After a Bluff-Daddy concert there is the wild pushing and
	shoving to get out, often fist fights on the stairs, even
	the possibility of seeing somebody get stabbed
Don't try to compare Bluff-Daddy with Beethoven
Bluff-Daddy reaches your soul, shakes you, makes you feel
	part of something greater than just music
Beethoven is the past when you had to think about
	what you're hearing instead of just feeling it
You can't compare Bluff-Daddy to Beethoven

WHO'S THAT KNOCKING?

Who's that knocking on my door?
Could it be she?
She coming back, back to say she was wrong, so wrong,
"What a mistake I have made," she will say. "You were
        right all along. You were the best thing in my life.
        With you and only you I found happiness."
"Will you take me back?" She will ask.
"Will you forgive me?" She will ask.
Please don't tell her that I've found another
Please tell her that I still love her, she cries.
Tears run down her cheeks
She is sorry, so clearly, so sincerely sorry.
I step back fearful that she will throw her arms around me,
Begging, begging for me to love her once again.
Begging, begging for me to forget that so painful past.
I stand firm but know that I shall once again give in.
I shall be that fool again, again that fool.
I so much want to believe we can love again.
We shall be together again.
The knocking at my door has stopped.
I feel relieved that I did not answer.
To not know that it was not her.

ROY SHIFRIN — BRONZE SCULPTURE
NOV.12-DEC.6 ALWIN GALLERY · LONDON
ROY SHIFRIN ESCULTURA NOV.14-DIC.6
TOM MADDOCK GALLERY · BARCELONA

CRICKETS

It was springtime, the field was alive with crickets
Clouds from the recent storm parted
And the light of the full moon sparkled on the wet grass as
      off a vast rolling sea
A sea waving to the song of crickets

So loud, they did not stop or pause or grow softer
To whom were they singing, who understood this so
      insistent song?
Was the moon above listening or the grasses bending and
      bowing in the breeze?

Or is it to me who stands here this night alone among them?
The moon went behind a cloud and there was silence
In the darkness have they stopped because it is my turn,
      my turn to sing to bring back the moon?
Are they thinking, you have come among us now you must sing?

I stood self-consciously at the edge of the sea of grass.
Timidly I started to sing, a song to the moon remembered from
      my childhood in Spain.

      Luna, Lunera, Cascabelera
      Ojos azueles, Cara morena

They didn't even wait for me to finish, for the moonlight
      returned and they joyously started to sing again
Perhaps the moon and crickets understand Spanish
Or maybe they too sing love songs to spring, from a childhood
      remembered near the sea, beside a field after the rain,
      below a full moon

SEA SONG

I feel such emotion
On returning to the ocean
To swim there with porpoise and whales
Abandoning my roots
And these dusty old boots
For a sleek fitting suit made of scales

Survival of the fittest I'll try
Asking no where, when, or why
Leaving all but to instinct and chance
Content to eat kelp
Expecting no help
In adapting to great nature's dance

No fear of wind, weather, or rain
Book-learning that addles the brain
Here in schools you just swim about
Perfection's no problem for fish
Nor wealth the ultimate wish
With etiquette just a thing fresh-fish flout

On a seabed I'll sleep
Oceanic dreams far, wide, and deep
For here is where everything began
I'll explore as I will
Copulate to my fill
Without guilt that I'll evolve into man

I will do nothing rash
Just a confident splash
Knowing the depth's where life truly belongs
Mankind's a blight on dry earth
With no sense of its worth
So sing out such sea savoring songs

POEM FROM THE SPANISH

Of you, of your love I did not understand
I could read you as a book, I believed
Put you upon the page so to hold you close
To have you there, mine bound between covers
There beside my bed, there beside me in bed
How I so selfishly believed, but I was wrong
Now I know, I know, I did not understand

I could write you as a book, a book of poems to have
          you love me, I believed
Rhyming upon the page as I would wish you to be
Explain away that why, a poetic why
Why I loved you and why you must love me and
          undoubtedly it would ever be
How I so selfishly believed, but I was wrong
Now I know, I know, I did not understand

Should you ever leave me I could simply erase you as a
      writer can rub out his lines
To undo, to unremember what I once read and wrote,
That you in prose or poetry but my words upon a page my
      portrait of you, at my discretion to be hung
      upon my heart
You who now I know were beyond my words, you were
      your own words, you your own work of art
How I so selfishly could not believe, but I was wrong
Now alone, now I know, I know, I did not understand

MOMENT IN TIME

Our past, the past, all but a moment in time
That past, so vast, so long ago, now just a moment
      in time
How I wanted, want to return, to have it back again
But no, it was and will ever be but a moment
And one can never return to such moments in time
No matter how much joy there was, or joy remembered,
      or believed remembered
It remains, will remain, but as a moment in time

You had such a starring roll in that moment
You spoke your lines so beautifully in those
      moments
One cannot say that they were not spoken true
For if anything too true, all too true
And I in that moment of time, for me it was always you,
      never anyone but you

In that moment of time
In memory, in that past was it always me?
Or was it simply never meant to be
Best not re-judge past moments of time
Surely then there was much joy
In memory it remains, will always remain
In memory, memories of those moments
Past, long past, so long ago, now just a moment in time

PAPER ROSES

There is nothing so dead as these paper roses
Faded red, pedals missing, dust dry stalks in a cracked bowl
      set upon the table
A "Still Life" artists might call it
But better called, "Life far too still"
Silent, thornless, no growth, no bees or butterflies about, no
      dew at dawn, no scent, no joy, just false
A false hope for spring, no danger in the picking, unsuitable
      as a gift of love or its memory
No, there is nothing so dead as these paper roses

A DARK RECTANGLE

A dark rectangle in this grassy field
A perfect cut opened in this manicured lawn
An opening to a below so rarely seen

I stop, ahead she runs to visit a family grave
I stop, but just to look down into this fresh opening
How deep and dark down there, how far from green grass
     and summer sun
Standing at the edge down there seems so far
Only the smell of freshly dug earth rising up
Surprising, it is not forbidding, not as I imagined
Not sad, no signs of loss or tears
Just an opened patch of earth prepared as a bed to lie upon

There is an urge to jump down — crazy; to see if
    it is as cool down there as it looks
No, I shall not jump. I only stand a long time looking
    down, thinking,

There far longer than life we all shall lie, perhaps with a stone,
     a carved name
I hear a name being called. There from out of the distant
     dark rectangle of stones?

It is she.
She is calling as she runs towards me from beyond
     the stones.
The sun blinding off her white summer dress, she is
     so alive
I step back and catch her in my arms.
Holding tightly to her I say, "Let this now today be
     as long as it can be."
She looks at me beside this dark rectangle wondering the
     meaning of this plea.

SHE

She stood on the stage above us
Tall, so thin, no breasts, no hips, short hair
    in a so simple black dress
Unsmiling, cold, as if detached from we who
    surrounded her looking up
Surely not a figure of beauty or desire, no the opposite

The orchestra grew quiet
She slowly stepped forward into the light and out from that
    so simple black dress, out from that austere body, out
    from parted lips flowed God in all his grandeur just
    as Mozart had heard Him
Sounds so beautiful, of love, of longing, of such sadness
I, who never cry, felt tears in my eyes
In that light she was beauty, was loveliness transformed by
    song into the ideal of desire
Someone to hold, to comfort, to love

I don't remember her name, I never heard or
    saw her again
But when I think of art and beauty, I hear her voice
Through my eyes and with my hands, I have made grand complicated
    art, I have made an art career
While remembering a so simple black dress, and that
    art at its most magical and glorious also comes by ear

BARCELONA OF
MY DREAMS

Barcelona of my dreams
Back, long back, when I was young with wonder and you
 an old rumbling rebelliousness under tyranny's heel.
Your walls aged and crumbling, dirty with fascist graffiti, alleys
 smelling of blocked drains and past horrors.
Grandeur consigned to be long passed through which
 dark, drab, crowds strolled away Sundays
Aimlessly on Ramblas, Avingudas, Eshamples, whispering
 in Catalan below street signs and marquees shouting
 out everything in enforced Castellano.
On the Paseo scant displays in the store windows, just the
 undervalued with the overpriced.
For me you were a peseta peasant; I, a shameless dollar king.
In that ragged time, censorship and caution flowered, and
 all news was officially good

In the movie houses or running on TV were the dubbed inanities
      of America's cultural worst.
Yet, the Mediterranean sun still shone, somewhere in secret
      Sardanas were danced, time quietly ticked, heads nodded
      sure that "Change" would be more than a sign in a tourist
      office window.

As I grew older you grew younger, "Change" came, real and swiftly,
Along with spring came savory smells sweeping out of cafes where
      men, women, huddled, heads close together, planning,
      plotting, creating their own Barcelona, a Barcelona to be.
And it came joyously and alive.
I stretched my arms, rubbed my eyes, yes outside it was true, it
      was a "un nuevo dia," as I called it.
But no it was, "un dia nou" as it would be called, written, and
      spoken in their Catalan.
And I, Barcelona's long Castilian lover, found myself awaking, but
      into their dream, a child again, and if to join them in play,
      to learn a new mother tongue.

FRIENDSHIP

I'm finally done with it
We have been friends since childhood but it's over
All those years of your recalling our days in High School and
       how you made all those varsity teams
How I too could have made a team if only I had not been so
       short and skinny
Your bragging in college how you understood the complicated
       String Theory, how quickly you solved the Sunday crossword,
       and always scored "genius" on IQ tests
Suggesting what I needed was to read more to improve my mind
Your monologues after college going on and on about yourself,
       barely able to even fake an interest in me
Yet, telling everyone that I was secretly jealous of you because
       you were earning so much more than I
Still whenever we went out to dinner you unfailingly let me pick up
       the check
And my girlfriends, you never liked any of them always saying
       that I could do better
When any one of them left me you consoled me by pointing
       out that clearly she felt herself too good for me
When I got married you said my wife was pleasant but, to be honest,
       frankly not attractive
When divorced and feeling so terrible you sympathized by telling
       me how beautiful and perfect she had been
You always pointed out that you were my only true friend, all the
       others were constantly saying terrible things behind my back
And flattering me that you saw me as that true friend in an
       emergency you knew you could always depend on

My emergency when I asked to borrow some money for a few days
  you said you never lend money because it only diminishes
  a friendship
Instead you advised me that I should learn how to better handle
  my finances so as not make a burden of myself
Yes, I'm finally done with it. It's over. And come to think of it,
  it never was.

A RICHER MAN

He lives his life not for love, fondness, friendship, or
        family - only gain
Never a thought of those out there or asking why
By fire, famine, flood, or fierce war there is death and pain
No, for his stocks rose today, and now as a richer man,
        surely he could never die.

URBAN HERMIT

He lives, if living is a lack of luxury
      or even necessities,
In one bare room, bare walls
With peeling paint from when he and this
      world were young
Now old, old floors dirty in unswept yesterdays
      with newspapers abandoned in its corners
Small bed unmade, there for sleep and
      sitting, perhaps to eat upon
While viewing the world through unwashed
      windows, where the sky is always
      streaked gray above a noisy street

His stove, single burner, a pot, a pan, bit of
      day-old bread called dinner
One bare bulb, one switch, one door through
      which no one visits

A drip then another in the cracked bathroom
      sink where he, along with waterbugs,
      dare to wash

This is a standard picture of poverty
A man alone in rags, alone in his room – tragic?
But no, here this man calculates, the bright light of his
      computer screen is his sun, moon, and god
He owns this room. He owns the whole building
He owns this prime real estate in the
      city center.

In the bank his account numbers in the millions
But he has only one thought, to speculate, to win
A longing beyond the desire for luxury, or what
      wealth can buy,
Life lived as a hermit deprived of only more
His dream, ever larger numbers at its core

CUTTING EDGE PHONE

I have it, the new,
So smooth hanging from my belt or warm inside
      my pocket, glowing in my hand
Shiny, rich in chips and circuits, a multi-colored
      screen that flashes to my commands
It rings, it clicks, quick connecting
      me to the world
I miss nothing
I know time by split seconds, news as
      it happens, all the wheres and whys I wish
My day to be neatly ordered
By night it never sleeps
I dare not move without it
More than necessity — it holds my past, future,
      pleasure, pulse and passion
I have this most versatile tool, a cutting edge tool
Yet surprisingly, how little of actual importance
      I do do with it

2G

It was 2G
I don't remember their names, they were the old couple who
      lived in apartment 2G
2G in a typical six-story apartment building in the South
      Bronx
Running down stairs after school, taking two at a time anxious
      to play outside with my friends,
Passing the second floor 2G's door would open and one of
      them would yell for me to stop making so much noise.
With them everything was always too much noise
Once a month an oil truck would come to fill up the building's
      tank parking by the curb with its motor running
2G would always open their window shouting for him to
      shut off the engine no matter how many times the
      shout came back that the engine had to be on
      to pump the oil
On Saturday evenings Angela and her boyfriend, who her
      parents didn't like, would hold hands under the
      street light and whisper affectionate things
      to each other
2G, I heard, would open their window above and throw
      water down on them
At noon on Saint Patrick's Day, by tradition the Collins brothers
      playing their fife and drum would march up the
      block from the Shamrock Bar.
As they passed under their window every year 2G would
      threaten to have them arrested if they didn't shut up.
2G even complained to the Monsignor about the Sunday
      bells of Sacred Heart church three blocks away.

Everyone at one time or another had been shushed or
    threatened with water by 2G
It was said that most of the neighbors on the third floor took
    their shoes off when home so that they wouldn't have
    2G knocking up from below all evening.
Over the years of my childhood it became just a part of living
    in the building.
One night at about eleven the street was filled with the roar
    of ambulances, police car sirens, shouts of medics,
    flashing lights, running feet, the sounds of
    an emergency
It was for Mr. 2G, a heart attack.
Quickly a crowd gathered as he was carried out.
Amid the noise and flashing lights as the stretcher passed out
    on the street everyone looked at one another and then
    all eyes instinctively went up to 2G's window,
    waiting for our being shushed and water thrown down
    upon us.

CITY DOG TELLS ALL

No, it's not easy to live in the city
Even harder to be a pet in the city, even worse a dog.
Condemned forever to wearing a leather collar around your neck
      where hangs tags certifying you are but a dog, state registered,
      numbered as a prisoner, noted free but only of various noxious
      diseases.
Perhaps on that leather hand painted a ridiculous name like Barney,
      Rasputin, or Bubbles depending on your owner's ego,
      economic status, or personal pretensions.

Always with a strong ring attached for securing that so symbolic
      statement of dominance, the leash.
Expecting without a doubt that you want to do as master wants to
      do, go out for a walk in rain or snow and accepting it as if a
      favor to me.
On seeing that leash expected to perform by prancing around in
      pseudo-joyous anticipation, wagging my tail in apparent
      surprise at such kindness, bark, bark, I say so that
      master smiles
As if one enjoys being dragged about with any sign of a will of my
      own resulting in hard pulls on my neck and shouts of those
      ridiculous words taught as if in some Nazi-like obedience
      school, "heel, heel, heel".
No concern if the path ahead is painfully icy or sun heated as
      the top of a stove, I must not complain but follow paws
      frozen or baked raw
While owner walks on oblivious well prepared for all weather, open
      shirt or woolen gloves and muffler.

And those very words "owner or master", terrible words whether
	referring to man or beast
Noting my position the total lack of respect for what might be
	important to me or my sensitivities.
Long ago neutered for their convenience, no natural selection in this
	household, no motherhood, fatherhood, sexual enjoyment,
	not for pets, so unseemly they say.
As for privacy, expected to perform my natural functions
	where master would never dare,
The local fire hydrant on the corner, over-used and never
	cleaned, out there were all can see
While being stood over, impatiently waiting for me to perform my
	other functions at their convenience with tissues or a plastic
	bag at hand to scoop it up as if something dirty and
	unnatural to be quickly dumped in a garbage pail
Meanwhile passersby look on with disapproving expressions,
	"why here, why on my street" in their eyes I see
	them thinking.
How demeaning. No, it is not easy to live in the city
Even harder to be a pet in the city, even worse a dog

Many a night I sense that this is not the life or place where I was
	designed to live.
If so why then these sharp teeth and claws, and those so un-pet-like
	doggy desires.
Somewhere deep in a dark memory I seem to recall a time beyond
	the feeding bowl and a world of concrete pavements
A time when there was the scent of the hunt in the air, the chasing
	of the fleeing deer and hounding the timid rabbit in his hole
Living with irregular eating habits, biting deep into living flesh,
	fresh food without that taste as from a tin can or cereal mush
	from a bag.

Such a time way back, when life was short and each and every
           day was an adventure
To eat or not, or to be eaten or not, mind always alert for the
           predator wolf in the brush or the keen eyed raptor above
           watching from the cliff
A world so different from lying bored in a cushioned basket with a
           sand box replacing the free forest tree or flowering bush
Those so strong memories of a wild past often return when they
           who own me expect I'll so docilely follow at master's heel.
What strong memories imagining the pleasure it would be to take
           a vicious bite out of that heel.
But no, I would only be thought un-natural, mad, hydrophobic, sent
           off to the pound and gassed
How did I degenerate into but a pampered pet, the play toy of an
           arrogant species that I am today?
When forest sounds, babbling brooks, bird songs, freedom were
           replaced by, "come, come boy, here good dog, good dog, sit
           up, up, beg, isn't that so cute?"
I have no idea, I'm only a dog, thought without my own feelings
           they're sure and happy with whatever I get.
No, it's not easy to live in the city.
Even harder to be a pet in the city, worse of all, as a dog.

WONDERFUL DAYS

Oh, how we hate progress
How we hate change
Those wonderful good old days
When we hunted mastodons with
      pointed sticks
Died of simple cuts and bruises, a fall
      or for no reason at all
When our only thoughts were of hunger, fear,
      and lust
The good old days

The wonderful good old days
When they labored lovingly planting seeds in
      rows tending the tender shoots
How we swept in and stole the harvest knowing
      we were the stronger, the survivors
Such natural order justified by our horned
      and helmeted gods
The good old days

The wonderful good old days
Hovels, mud, and rags, the city a place of
        infestation, death, obedience, and might
As we looked down from the rocky citadel, armed,
        and ready, rulers by divine right
The good old days

The wonderful good old days
When all worshiped the only true and loving god
And those we burnt for misbelief or seeking
        knowledge beyond blind faith.
Every man knew his role and place or else
The good old days

The wonderful good old days
The factory and the loom, bound to production
        by the fear of hunger and cold
The world calling out there for our goods,
        our labor, our coins, our conquest
Our market places worshipping an idol of gold
The good old days

The wonderful good old days
Steam, industry and commerce, a vast new
        world where money's king
We the few eat well, and in the streets and beyond
        our shore, the hungry believing poor who
        god will eventually reward at no cost to us
The good old days

The wonderful good old days
When change was promised but cautious,
        cosmetic and slow

Dressed up in the fine phrases, democracy,
    technology and progress
While we the consistently financial few, have
    computer programmed you to believe
    much has changed
From those good old days we knew

HE WOKE UP

He woke up – his hand didn't work
So he ignored it
To get out of bed with one hand was possible
Perhaps even easier – and no one would
      expect him to wave in greetings

He woke up – his foot didn't work
So he ignored it
To go hopping about was not too hard
Slower - but he was not in a rush to arrive anywhere

He woke up – his eyes didn't work
So he ignored it
The sun was always of too bright colors, too vivid
Better- to imagine reality unbothered by what is there

He woke up – his heart didn't work
Hard to ignore but he did
He had no love of life, no love for his fellow man
Easy – being heartless did not feel strange

He woke up – his mind didn't work
Wasn't hard to ignore that
No thought of today, tomorrow, all whys or when
And so – he hobbled to the capitol believing himself
      particularly well suited to govern

THE END OF THE WORLD

The world will end
Destruction will be total by atomic fire or fall of brimstone
        or great flood, or famine and frost
It will happen suddenly at Armageddon or maybe South Los
        Angeles since afterwards it will be hard to tell

Just an empty spinning globe
Of course, as prophesized, God's chosen will first have been
        "raptured" up to heaven
Elephants, apes, whales, birds, fish, insects, bushes, branches,
        all one by one up and away

The silence of birdsongs, whale songs, the rustling of leaves,
        the buzzing and humming of insects
All this will not be noticed by those not chosen, not "raptured"
They shall be too busy working to save their money or their
        souls, in that order
All happening so slowly, an elephant here, a flock of birds
        there, a few less fish, who'll missed them, or a forest,
        a river, a ridge
That end will be exactly as had been predicted, mankind's biblical
        destiny rudely fulfilled

And the deity, him, her, or they will brush away the dust, open
        a new book to a blank first page
And on it, in an exquisite hand, once again write, "In the beginning,"
He, she, or they will pause for a moment and smile, confident
        that in perhaps a billion years or so the distant heirs of these
        recently "raptured", patiently, more wisely, will once
        again wish to continue the story.

HEREAFTER

The end of the world came as all faiths foretold
Believers greeted the news with joy and laughter
Be they the meek, timid, rash, or brazen bold
Anticipating that long promised rich hereafter

That new world fresh and fine under a forever sun
The chance to start the whole thing over
In a paradise where forests thrive and rivers run
Through broad fields flowering with clover

In peace together the lion with the timid deer
Above birds fill the sky with song
And though one may listen, one shall not hear
A cry of pain, or fear, nor hint of something wrong

In this new land shall live
Mankind but a new perfected breed
Generous in nature to both take and give:
From each his best, for each all that he may need

Over the people of this holy place
Shall rule God, the grand and just
Aglow with radiance on a loving face
Engendering confidence and complete trust

Such a world remade in every part
No more rich and no more poor
All people living for love and art
So joy and happiness are there secure

Alas, all the above might prove a lie
Surely it could not be God's plan
To have us await this promised by and by
While here and now God has man as wolf to man

GLORIOUS NIGERIA.COM

Oh, glorious Nigeria
Vast far-off land somewhere across the sea,
     Africa I think.
Land of generosity, land of giving, great
     cornucopia of goodness
Madam Olgamonga in her email writes,
"Dear sir or madam, I know that I can trust
     you."
Such wisdom, I don't know her but she is wise
     enough to know that I am truly trustworthy.
"My husband has just died."
How sad and she wishes to share this personal
     tragedy with me.
"He was the president of the Nigeria National Bank"
Here is no night washwoman with access to a
     computer. She was married to a man of
     distinction.
"My late husband was in charge of all the funds for
     the Bamumbo Railroad."
I was right, a man of distinction.
"The Bamumbo Railroad has gone out of business."
A double tragedy, both for this poor woman and the
     Bamumbo Railroad.
"The forty billion dollars remaining in their account
     was left in my late husband's name."
At least she will not starve out on the street or perhaps
     it's an unpaved road.
"It is all legal"
Would I expect otherwise of such a devoted wife?

"If you would be kind enough to help me claim
        this sum I would be willing to give you
        twenty percent."
Think of it, money for me. I would help her without
        thought of reward.
Madam, tell me how I can assist you.
"Please send to this postal address one thousand dollars
        so that I can buy alligator shoes for walking into
        the bank and get the necessary documents to sign."
Sad, how terribly expensive such things are in her country.
        But, the wife of such a distinguished man must
        certainly appear in proper attire.
"God bless you for sending the money. The documents will
        soon be in the mail."
Much later the sixteen year-old son of Madam Olgamonga
        writes to tell me that his dear mother was killed and
        eaten by an alligator and that it was most certainly
        the fault of the shoes that I had bought her.
Was I responsible? And is not twenty five thousand dollars
        for a funeral a bit expensive for a woman who has been
        eaten?
I sent the son only ten thousand.
He graciously thanked me and writes that eight billion has
        been transferred into my name.
But before I can claim it the Nigeria National Bank requires that
        I pay to him the customary fifty thousand dollar
        estate tax."
I am forwarding to you, dear reader, this tragic poem in the hope
        that you may be willing to help me pay that required fee
        thereby honoring Madam Olgamonga's dieing request.

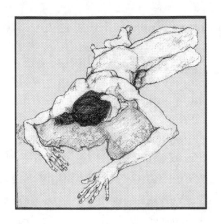

EXCERPTS

(WITH WILLIS' NOMENCLATURE) FROM DR. HARRISON'S 1807 DISSERTATION ON THE DISSECTION OF THE HUMAN BRAIN

Note the Basilar Artery channeling the most vital of humors
Carrying them as they flow from the Corpus Internum
Rich in hopes, thoughts of love, throbbing with desires
So noticeable in the pulses at the wrist engendering the motivation
    to reach out, touch, embrace, and possibly kiss

Nearby is the Pontine Artery, it's name resonant as a bridge
Perhaps the bridge between those clearly visible shores that note
    the sensible and irrational?
Where mankind's tides ebb and flow as if the rich, dark, and rosy
    waters of war and peace,
Humors of natural aggression mixing with the milk of
    human kindness

Then there is the Ophthalmic Artery suggesting something to do
        with sight
Linking the eye's orbs carrying the many currents of beauty seen
        in the world
Such a flow allowing us to savor the sweet liquor of color
As found in pastoral scenes, the beloved's features or that sylvan
        stream that engenders the arts on its bubbling course

Here the Hypophyseal Artery, beating a course above the others
Through it runs the higher drives of bravery and action
That which powers the muscled arm to firmly hold the sword
Exhibiting the determination to triumph even if red gushes
        from the open wound

Animating the large Perforating Artery, that most noble river of
        determination
Which in spite of all wounds, distant leakage from either
        artery or vein, wills one to fights on
Enriching the desire to strike back, to perforate the foe
As if a cold determination that will not allow rest until revenged

Lastly we have the Thalamostriate Artery flowing flood with
        those fluids that joins the meaning of the world with
        man's thoughts towards his purest poetic nature
Here fixing the centers of love, beauty, honor, right and
        reason, with its beats so clearly linking heart to brain

Or as such as I can surmise from but these most cursory
        observations placed upon this page.

MAGI

As once in the Bible so here today three modern Magi came
They had traveled far and long
They, too, came seeking a newborn babe
They, too, had gifts for the child, also things very
      valuable but essentially useless

Carrying such heavy burdens they too will travel long and far,
      seeking a newborn, who as if by child's play, with a
      wave of a commanding hand be able to
      bringing world peace and universal joy
But times had changed even in the holy land of the Bible
In this modern age all was clearly more complicated, much more
      difficult, than blind faith bringing easy solutions
There were now novelties called democracy, feminine equality,
      terrorism, mullahs, Zionists, petroleum concessions, and
      serious environmental concerns
Yes, of course there was still corruption where valuable but
      useless gift might be able to influence important
      politicians and provide access to such a child
Even a world of peace and joy, still very much sort, but
      now with different interpretations in different lands,
      in different tongues, and thought attainable by
      vastly different means

As in the Bible, Magi, whatever meaning or authority that title might
      hold, could today return
Traveling on, hot under their heavy loads, crossing foreign lands
Still hoping to see peace and joy the easy way, with gifts to a child
      born with a magical commanding hand

Yet they too will doubt whether such a child exists, or could have
    ever existed, especially one today to be found in a poor
    peasant's hovel, the child of illiterate ethnic parents
Or, if world peace, or their offerings of gifts, valuable but
    essentially useless, would help make it so, any more
    than those Magi who searched by starlight so long ago.

WHOSE GOD?

If lambs had a God
They would pray, "O' mighty lord of the universe,
    by your goodness keep us safe in your love
    and laws from the hungry lion's jaws."

If lions had a God
They would pray, "O' mighty lord of the universe,
    in your goodness provide us lambs to eat for you
    who made hunger made us crave meat."

In this world some are as the lamb, and some the lion,
    we can plainly see.

So whose God is it?

    For the same God for both it cannot be.

ROY SHIFRIN'S *The Great American Horse* NOV. 21st 2003

MY WORLD

If I were to remake the world
The sky, sun, mountains, grasses and
     all nature's trees
As well as rocky shores, sandy beaches, and of
     course the vast and roaring seas

If I were to fill up that world
With bees, bugs to whales, both grain eaters
     and the fiercest carnivores
Who live their lives in great green forests
     or far from those rocky shores

If I were to make each unto itself a world
Putting forth nuts, seeds, cubs, and kin up
     to humans giving birth
All driven by an internal desire to make of
     themselves the more and
     populate my earth

If I were to place reason in this world
For to see, observe, to contemplate from the
        grains of sand up to the sky
Desiring to know all wherefores, all whens,
        always asking why

If I were to pick a species for such a gift
One to use it wisely, lovingly, for now to
        ever after
High on that list would be one who first
        I had given an appreciation of laughter

WEAR IN THE WORLD?

Where in the world is that world I wore?
My hat now covers a bald spot as if a melting pole
My worn shirt once floral and bright now bleached
      bare and brown as the dry Sahara
My wool sweater lovingly knit now heartlessly pulled
      threadbare as a clear-cut Amazon
And my raincoat, as protection from acid rains, cracked and
      torn useless against storms that sting my cheeks
Pants stained and muddy from trudging through fields
      sprayed dead and long fallow
Socks with toes stuck through, from dipping into dead seas
      once bright blue now of algae and floating fish
In scuffed shoes, so dressed without a home, I march on
      alongside those who also now wear nothing
      more to loose.

GOD'S DAY

When God on TV comes down to Earth
Into the grand plaza where the many thousands wait
He is of course suitably dressed
A flowing cloak of many colors tailored by well-known
      fashion designers
Of such craftsmanship bearing large wondrous golden embroidered
      halos on the lapels each
Surrounding life-like portraits of himself so exquisitely capturing
      his beatific features
On his worldly head a white silk skullcap
Surly stitched by the dexterous hands of many virgins from
      that nunnery well guarded behind locked doors set high
      atop the surrounding hills
On his feet purple leather slippers made from the softest
      skins of lambs sacrificed in strict accordance
      with holy ritual
See in these slippers how gracefully he steps into the
      bulletproof motorized cart to be praised by all those
      shouting and waving as he passes before them
The official guards armed and dressed in many-colored medieval
      designs press forward before the cart making a way
      for it to pass
He of course stops to perform that humble ritual of washing
      the feet of twelve picked at random heretics before
      they are returned to their prison cells
Ahead, set on a fine white tablecloth in a silver salver,
      six small fishes ready and well prepared to symbolically
      feed the world

God, his heavy tasks now done in his majestic manner circles
        around the plaza bestowing on all from radiant eyes the
        wisdom that they are seeing the carnal stand-in for
        the supreme being
Then with colorful guards and bulletproof cart he returns to his
        rooms in a most majestic palace for a deserved rest.
The screen goes blank and the Vatican TV logo appears.

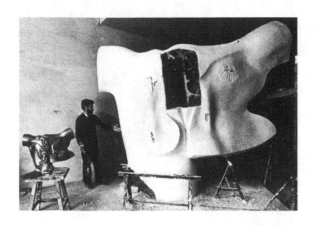

JOGGING AS GOD

Yesterday, jogging around the lake
Before me on the path a circle of noisy crows
Pecking with their long sharp beaks
At what appeared to be a stone.

Approaching, it was not a stone
But a small turtle tightly tucked in its shell
A shell the crows were determined to open,
To crack open for inside they knew was food

On my approach they turned, their eyes staring
At me; was here but a passing jogger or something else?
I, them, and even the encased turtle
Waited to find out if God glorious had arrived.

The crows suspected and flew up into the branches
Of a nearby tree to watch.
In that silence of no longer pounding beaks
The small turtle did believe and extended its legs

To dash, to escape, to reach the nearby lake, to live.
No longer just a passing jogger out for exercise,
Now thrust upon me the power to hold worlds
	within my hand.
To create either a miracle of salvation or manna for
	the watching hungry?

Interfere or not with the natural order of things?
I, a Solomon in sneakers, would judge; live or die.
Above the clouds parted, an ethereal shaft of sunlight
	lit the path ahead
As a breeze, cool and beckoning blew over
	that nearby lake.

THREE SONS

The father, off for a beach vacation to where the wealthy go
Called his three sons together and spoke to them as so...
You, my eldest, I entrust a million dollars, to my second, half that
     sum, and one hundred thousand to you my youngest one
When I return I hope to learn your business skills and see
     how well you each have done
As soon as he left the eldest invested his million in the industries
     of war
There through conflicts, selling to every side he swiftly made
     a million more
The second took his sum and lent it at high fee to the
     desperate poor
And when they could not repay he foreclosed, sold what
     little they had and made half a million more
The youngest placed his sum in a vault where it would be safe
     and sound though there no profit would be found
At last tanned from many days of sea and sun the father returned
     anxious to see how each son had done

The eldest proudly returned the million and the million more
      saying through war, death and destruction see how I
      have added to your store
Good son, wise son, the father said, in finance all compassion you
      denied, come eat and drink at my table and sit close here
      by my side
The second son placed his half million on the table and the half
      million more
Saying see how I have cleverly extorted from the poor and by
      their hardship I have added to your store
Good son, wise son, the father said, in finance all compassion you
      denied, come eat and drink at my table and sit here
      by my side
The youngest returned the one hundred thousand all neatly bound
      from the vault where it had lain all safe and sound
Father he said, I return what is yours without pain and profit to
      you I can assure
That unlike my bothers it has brought no death, or heavy hardship
      to the poor
Father, you are a man who I have heard speak often of our loving
      God and how in his path you go
So I thought your noble nature you would wish for all the world
      to know
The father scowled, roared, struck his youngest, and disowning
      him drove him from his door
Foolish son be gone, God and morality are just fine words meant
      to hide that which here we worship more.

SHE DID NOT COME

I left outside a saucer of warm milk
    But she did not come

I hung a honeycomb on a thread over the door
As the seer said, I also rubbed lavender on its frame
Put a candle in the window where one can clearly see the flame

    But she did not come

As in folk tales I placed a jar of lightning bugs each one sparking
    its desire for a mate on the front porch
Beside it a caged nightingale to sing all through the night
Hung a mirror up above to reflect upon the path moonlight

    But she did not come

The astrologer assured me it would be in April but was unsure
    the date
The holistic healer said first I must purify myself mind, body,
    and soul
She who could sense spirits predicted she'd come preceded
    by the church bell's toll

    But she did not come

Better to chant those complicated words the Indian guru taught
    that never fail
Stick a pin into a phone book and meditate on the name, let
    random chance prevail

At the computer shop they told me to send my picture
        and Email addressed, "to she who I'll adore"

    But still, still she did not come

In desperation I write these words. Should she reads them
        she will see I am sincere
Ready for love, and still patiently waiting here

POOR AND WEALTH

Mine is that love sincere
Growing the greater day by day
And nothing do I hold more dear
Then these words to you I say,

My feelings I do not hide
Though your parents think them untrue
Poor, yes I am poor that cannot be denied
But I am and will always be in love with you

"True-love cannot exist between poor and wealth,"
Your father tells you this I know,
That my feelings are for gain not for you yourself.
That's false! False and you must tell him so

Tell him all his riches we forsake to share a simple fate
And only by our love and labors shall we dine
Not with his golden forks on China plate
But if plastic — as of the rarest gold that from lover's eyes
          does shine

GREED

Today to understand our world
This basic fact you must believe
That humanity was born and has
      evolved through greed

Friendship, travel, art and song
Wife, trust, worship of the gods above
All nothing compared to amassing those
      possessions that we love

Clearly, more is more and less is less
It is the fool who for good works crave
Ignoring the innate satisfaction of going
      richest to the grave

True, bones eventually molder
Even grand monuments turn to dust
Be confident, history honors greed and those
      who for more did lust

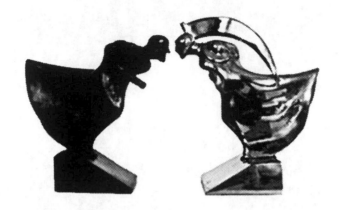

TO THE BARREN PLAIN

Dark is the place between still and sleep
Where thoughts unharnessed go riding.
Memories of past love where willows weep
And I in their shade lie hiding.

The withered branch, the beetle's bore,
Heartwood where remorse flows free
In thoughts of her whom I did adore
And believed that she adored me.

In love I saw that sapling green
To a great oak grow unbounded.
Among its leaves birds sang unseen
Their songs of joy resounded.

But her love proved to be untrue
My oak by rain and wind uprooted.
Such sturdy trees are but far and few
And I? To the barren plain best suited

THE STREAM

A river runs outside my door
Wide and deep and cold
On the other side a wondrous shore
Or so I have been told.

A land of fruit trees ripe and green
Fig, apple, plum and pear
Where hunger's never known or seen
Or so say those who write of there.

The sun lies warm upon that land
Summer, fall, winter, spring
With tenderness from every hand
Or so in song musicians sing.

Love is light and given free
The rose, lily, violet sweet
There loneliness can never be
Or so tell travelers that you meet.

Not gold but mind they do revere
Poems, music, all the arts
Beauty rich to see and hear
Or so boast they about such parts.

But, I will not try to swim that stream
Likely there one will only find
Words from a poet's flowing dream
Of wishful words writ from his mind

RETURNED HOME

When I return home
And you have returned home
We shall sit across from one another
      and speak.
You shall say things of little import
While I shall speak of great profundities
      which you find of little import.
The sun will set.
You will turn on the lights
I will lower the shades
The TV says it's cold out but as always
      you have no opinion.
I set a fire feeding the furniture into
      the flames
Then the curtains your mother gave us
The plastic flowers that do nothing but
      gather dust
The rarely opened book of family photos
Then the letters, the bills, receipts
      and deeds
You will smile or is it a smile?
I cry, "fire", dial 911, you call for help.
But we both know that help will not come.
All this shall run through my mine as it
      has done so often before
And your's? I don't really know what
      you think or imagine
As we sit across from one another
      and speak. Or is it silence
When I return home
And you have returned home?

SHE WHO WENT A YEARNING

Where is the you of late I knew who now acts all a yearning
For true love to find with your heart and mind in great
       passion there a burning

Be he pauper or prince or whoever since you're sure he'd be
       better than I
Seeing me as not cool just a drab dull fool when viewed
       through your cynical eye

But no better you'll find than what you're leaving behind here
       right here at home
It's a delusion you're under a real major blunder giving me
       up on the off chance to roam

Before saying your good-byes first open your eyes and see I am
       unfair to blame
Throwing me away for far better you say then to live this life
       dull and tame

It's your last chance, you insist that same same-old to resist living
       day after day being bored
Saying better to act, be bold, before you're too old to find real
       love not this sad make-do fraud

Wait, what about me, are you content to see me being left here
       abandoned, alone

We have long been as one is this what you want undone has your
        heart turned suddenly to stone?

"Yes", you reply, saying with a conscience so light it makes it
        all right to go off seeking a future of fun
Without care if some think you a bitch, you a true selfish witch
        doing what you say just has to be done

Wait, that can't be what you mean just a childish pipe dream
        please let's again give it a try
I'll change in all ways it will be as those exciting old days, are you
        listening? - the door slams. That can't be your final good-bye?

FREE FREE ME

"No, she said" I don't love you
I haven't love you for the past
          fifteen years
Yes, we have been married, slept every
          night in each other's arms
Used words like love and adore
          But, I haven't really loved you, you became
          "make do" nothing more
It was him, that imaginary him alone, my
          heart was destined for
He was and is the love of my life
To you I am what I was called, your wife
You believed our children are yours, of your
          seed, bred, born, and true
Technically so - sex served my need
Brought me joy, the pleasure imagining of it not being you
I dream the day shall come soon, the end of this
          month the latest, maybe two
Dreaming with him I shall then go away
To start my life over, to start anew
And the children, the house and car
          what of them you ask?
I paid those many years of suffering, playing the
          family role as my task
Free, free, I am entitled to be free
Mother, a wife always bored as hell with you
At last I shall be free, free...to be an imagined me

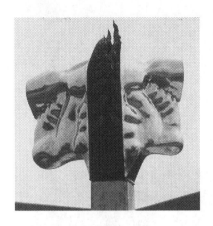

GOURMAND'S CREED

I think I have a stomachache
Perhaps what I ate was a mistake
Shellfish, fries, corned beef and slaw
Wine and beer and even more.

Perhaps tomorrow I'll be wise
And listen to those doctor's lies?
Only eating what I should
All those things we're told are good.

Low in cholesterol and sugar free
Rich in vitamins A, B, C, and E
Anti-oxidants, high fiber, soy
The heart-wise diet, cardiologists enjoy.

But can one live for good health alone
Condemned that for culinary joys one must atone?
No! My gourmand's creed rejects such sham,
"I eat — and don't give a damn."

NOTHING IS EVER GUARANTEED

Nothing is ever guaranteed — not spring
But the birch tree believes, puts forth buds
  and takes a chance
Birds fly north believing, they too
  take a chance
While the snow still lies in sunless places
  the grass unfolds its matted self to
  also take that chance
Spring is never guaranteed but it shall come
And Love?
Love certainly is never guaranteed but it too
  has put forth new leaves, unfolding,
  growing new and green, believing
So take a chance, take my hand and
  take that chance

TIME OUT OF MIND

Where was that time when one didn't think of time
When today followed past todays fearless of becoming
      yesterday and even less fearful of being thought
      as tomorrow
Again was truly again, mornings saw the same unchanging
      face in the mirror
All that seemed necessary to keep it so was to shave,
      some soap and water, and for her, a comb and lipstick
Beyond the windows, over breakfast, bright skies followed bright
      skies, below a wide view of sea and sand, day in day out,
      as it must have been at the beginning of the world, only
      Trilobites were missing
She and I, in a time noted in moments, as moments were meant
      to pass, slowly and unnoted
Noted now only in snapshots, black and white and yellowing
      of her holding a kitten
I, in faded color, on the beach pointing to a driftwood log

Humming over lunch to favorite pop songs playing on the radio
      if reception was clear
And dinners always eaten under a dark star-filled sky tasty as
      memories out of time, in a time without worry
Were we ever really concerned about money, or distant wars,
      death, another man or woman, a feared rival, or that
      mysterious pain in the side?
So sure that days would remain as days had been, no reason
      to think of the future, or so we so thought then
Do you still remember that wonderful time, when that old rusted
      pendulum clock we found on the beach, always reading
      4:14, hung as but decoration there on our wall?
And it never occurred to us to fix or rewind it.

YOUR HAT

You
Every morning I awake alone, open my eyes,
Look at the dresser where your hat still lies
And think, "What shall I do?"

Just a chance meeting in the noisy uproar
Of that Christmas party I felt obligated to attend
Leaving, those drunks asked, "going friend?"
As I pushed towards the front door

Laughing one of them placed on my head a hat,
A furry Russian thing. I said, "it's not mine,"
"It's cold outside", one said, "take it, on you it looks fine"
Standing like a tartar in Red Square. I heard, "Stop,
        you'll not get away with that"

It was you from across the room, "Don't let that hat-thief go,
There's atomic secrets sewn inside." You came up to me and
        smiling said, "I saw what happened, please,
It may look better on you, but it's mine and without it my
        ears will freeze."
We laughed. Though the fur was fake, it was true love at first
        sight, and so

I knew one couldn't take a chance and leave such a love to fate
I asked, "Can I invite you for coffee, there's a cafe nearby
Where it's quiet and we can exchange atomic secrets as spy to spy?
There 'till closing, I remember it was magical that first date

136

In a week we were living together, talking of all the exciting
        things we planned
To do together, lovers in the city, a coming spring and never
        again to be alone
Such laughter and joy who would have thought, or known
That it was to end, end in such a way, and so close at hand

That hat was our joke, I'd ask. "Which do you love more, it or me?"
For you wore it every night, most often nothing else, to bed
I'd remove it, and your answer wordlessly was so clearly said
Yet after, you held on to it so tightly. I wondered, a quirk?
        but said nothing, let it be

All that winter though I held you close you said how you
        always felt cold
Clutching that hat against your heart, even in sleep you
        held it so
For it hid a secret more terrible than atomic, now
        was I to know
You only said, "Hold me, love me now as if our 'now'
        will never grow old."

It was the start of spring, warm and green, the phone call, words
        I hear again and again
The paramedic, "It was her heart, everything we tried.
She just collapsed on the subway – "tell him I love him", was all
        she said before she died."
That hat there upon the dresser, fake fur, true love,
        a time so short, such pain

HIM

As a small child I remember that they called him "faggot"
Made his life a misery, beatings that left him black and blue.
I joined in with them shamelessly
Not in anger, I had no idea what "Faggot" was but fearful if I
  didn't I would be thought a "Faggot" too

The bigger boys said he was something strange, dangerous,
  a sinner
If you became his friend he would turn you into one as well
You would do things of which they only smiled to one another
Saying that for what he did there was reserved the deepest
  depths of hell

To me he didn't seem so bad; he was even good at sports,
And the girls liked him, maybe they thought him handsome,
  or because he didn't tease them as did we?
But he had joined the other side, liked to draw, adult music,
  was good at school

Could the older boys be jealous? Was not rough, tough, and
    teasing girls, what real men were meant to be?

My mother told me it was wrong to treat him so.
What did she expect? I so wanted to be part of the pack,
    so I told her I would stop — I lied.
One evening the older boys caught him in the alley, tore his
    clothing and with cigarettes badly burnt the "Faggot"
I never saw him again. There were lights and sirens, whispers,
    and the story, I don't know if even true — that in his
    room he cut his wrists and died.

THE VOYAGER

My mother was dieing
Not unexpected, just the swiftness unexpected
Old, frail, her body had long held tightly to life long after
       her mind had resigned itself to death
I was not home when the hospital called so they called my
       daughter, her grandchild.
She left work and rushed to the hospital

My mother lay in an empty room, just a bed, a chair, a machine
       softly clicking to the beat of her heart, while on its
       screen green numbers displayed a fading life
My daughter sat in the chair holding the hand that as a baby once
       held her
Those long fine fingers now small, wrinkled, cold.
Stroking that hand, my daughter quietly spoke to she who lay
       as if asleep, spoke to let her know, if she could know,
       that she was not alone.

I like to believe that my mother was dreaming there in
       that quiet room.
Dreaming that she who never traveled was aboard a great ship,
       young and beautiful again.
There beside her was my father, alive, handsome, so much in
       love with her.
The sea breeze blew through her hair, my father, a long
       ago traveler on that ship, held her tightly.
No mechanical clicks of pulse but the distant cries of
       gulls high, very high overhead telling of a ship soon
       to put out to sea.

Feeling the stroking of her hand, gentle as the waving of
	hankies by those far below, old friends, family, all now
	smiling, so happy, looking up, calling, wishing the loved
	travelers well on that so far a journey
And there below her son waving and crying, her grandchildren,
	her granddaughter holding tightly to the hand not wanting
	to let go.

The clicking of the gulls grew silent. Slowly the anchor was
	weighed, the captain took the wheel, the great prow
	turned oceanward, the green numbers noting wind
	and tide went dark.
Still in my daughter's hand lay the hand of the voyager. While I,
	too far off to again hold that hand, would be left upon a
	distant shore with only memories of she who so lovingly
	captained our small ship, slowly disappearing beyond the horizon.

FOREVER

Death "must" come to all they say – true, but why "must"
Could we not live forever?
Life lived without a wrinkle, no white hairs, body fit, no
      stoop or sag or shortness of breath
Time to waste, spent foolishly, putting off until
      tomorrow what we could do today
True love lasting not until death do we part but only 'til
      we part friends, without tears, no regrets, nor
      broken hearts, just the new him or her of dreams

On the other hand
Why then children, changing diapers, their food and board,
      schooling, when in the end they will leave home, never
      call, show little regard for you those parents who seem
      to always be around, were and are
While they expect our lifetime sense of responsibility for them who
      too will live forever

And meanwhile
Slaving away at an eternal job, day in day out, every morning
　　responsibly raising from sleep, painfully begrudgedly,
　　seemingly forever and it is all for what?
The constant climb up the corporate ladder, carefully saving
　　your salary or cleverly investing in stocks and bonds to
　　have more than what you could ever spend

But why?
Only looking forward to some enforced retirement to make way for
　　the ambitious young who want your job and will work for less.
Given that gold watch as a good-bye with the promise of golden
　　years to spend idling away in a forever by the sea, the
　　golf course, day in day out

Death clearly has something to say for itself, if "must" only leaves
　　such choices for you and me
Life eternal, while sounding good might in the end prove a serious
　　liability

CANCER A LA AMERICAN

Cancer, what a fearful word
For a disease that's most absurd

Sensible cells grow at fixed rates
While the Cancer cell proliferates

They refuse to live by healthy rules
The body's defenses it plays for fools

Attacking livers, lungs, perhaps the spleen
Or other organs vital, unseen

Fortunately doctors have the MRI
So into your innards they can pry

Seeing the anomalous image strange
Where flesh to foe has made that change

Then with wondrous laparoscopic devices
And at outrageous fees and prices

They cut the bad things all away
Shipped off for biopsy without delay

Such joy when they say you're as good as new
And smiling hand the bill to you

Cancer, what a fearful word
It can even kill you when you're cured

I DREAMT

I dreamt of you last night
As I've dreamt so often before
Once again I held you tight
No fear, or care of what was wrong
      or what was right
In love with you once more

That joy of being in love again
A love that knew no rest
No sad longings or pain
Or tears, dark days, cold winds, or
      bitter rain
Just those days I remember best

You tell me you could not stay away
No matter how hard you tried
Your life was empty day after day
Until we would be together, embrace, and
      you could say,
"I can not live without you by my side."

This dream, so real, goes on and on
As endless as love's pleasures seem
Our past unhappiness all dead and gone
All just anticipation - then that fierce
      morning's light fell upon
My opening eyes, and I again
      awaken from that dream

YOU ARE BEAUTIFUL

You are beautiful.
Right now so beautiful.
You show me a picture of when you were young
Tall and thin, long light brown hair, fair smooth skin,
Smiling for the camera or perhaps for him
        who held the camera
But you are now not happy.
You tell me that you must lose ten pounds.
That your hair is too short and there are traces of gray.
Saying, see what gravity has done to your breasts, arms, thighs
There are now small wrinkles around your eyes
You would never dare wear those tight jeans now
Nor dare smile before a camera knowing what it would show,
        the truth you say.
It is twenty years later and you are not the same.
Yet, in my twenty-year-older eyes you are even more beautiful
It's not flattery but true
What you see as imperfections is what I love
Those years written on our bodies have been well spent.
Together time's beauty will be ours forever, youth's beauty
        is only lent.

A SCARY NURSERY TALE

As darkness starts to fall
Patents to their children call —
You must get ready, no time to play
For we must rush upon our way
It's coming soon what dawdlers fear
At evening when bedtimes near
That thing, with delight, surely would
Dine on naughty children if it could
Its favorite dish I cannot lie
Are those to bed who whine and cry

Listen — I hear that fearful wail
Of the furry red-plumed Scarytail
You may ask, should I fear
When Scarytails are coming near?
Yes, with their tails a red so bright
Long and furry, what a fright
Wriggling it just where you'd think
Making tired eyes to rub and blink
If you say, "I won't sleep, not me."
Then without a doubt you'll see
A sight that makes non-sleepers quake
And wish that they were not awake

Horrors — it might pop up beneath the sheet
Looking for children's toes to eat
You must be brave, upon your face
No sign that eating toes is a disgrace
They get very angry if you're rude

Refusing them their proper food
Toes like your they've seldom seen
So pink and soft such high cuisine

To escape — quickly dream your toes are cold
Or from smelly socks six days old
It still may sniff and give a test
It tickles but lying very still is best
You'll see with sleepy eyes its nose is blue
And it has more than one but less than two
With one great eye above its noses
Fierce and naughty it never closes
On his lip's — see that vicious sneer
With sharp teeth from ear to ear
Hands with claws and nails most long
Oh so terrible, but don't get me wrong
You can be saved if it hears you snore
Such sleeper's sounds they most adore
You will be surprised as well you should
Around the dreaming child they turn to good
They sing, they dance, and that's your cue
To do the things brave dreamers do

Get all ready, get all set
Dream that Scarytail's in a fishing net
When caught, they may get angry but seldom bad
Most often they just get sad
Should it plead and start to wail
You must take it to the local jail
There they'll put it in a box
Held closed with many chains and locks
Even sadder it will sit and cry
Head in hands and wonder why
It was thought so bad and mean

Scarytails are not what they seem
I confess — toe eating monsters aren't true
To scare naughty children they're meant to do
So if in your dreams one should appear
Have no worry have no fear
From below your blanket loudly shout
"See, I'm fast asleep so just get out."

FORCED TO KNOCK

I stand before the door where death resides,
A visitor for the first time
Covering up my fears
In this rationalization set in rhyme.

Doctors say there is a worm that eats within
Seeking a core that if reached I die
And there is nothing, nothing to be done
But cling to a belief that all their tests but lie.

If not my life hangs by a so slender branch
Yet, when last I looked I stood a sturdy tree
An evergreen lit with merry Christmas lights
No thought the plug might be pulled on me.

About death, sure I knew that others die
I've seen their tombstones row on row
But passed without a thought of them
More important what to wear and where to go.

Now, I am being forced to knock upon that door
Hoping its occupant is out and I can return home
To laugh that it was all a misdiagnosis, a mistake
And I can burn this page and forget all about
      this poem.

YOUR FACE

I can't recall your face it was so long ago
You were beautiful, I remember that.
Men on the street would turn to look at you
I so clearly remember that, our exciting beginning, those first
     months together when everything was new.
How much we laughed, shared the same love of music, art,
     and politics.
Together in museums, at concerts, marching with
     banners in protest, and our travels
That bitter cold night in Canada sitting so
     close, kissing before the log fire, the
     smell of your perfume, your soft lips
And Florida at four in the morning, the darkened
     hotel pool, we swam, our bathing suits hanging on the railing
The Louve in Paris when the museum guard threatened to arrest
     you for taking a flash picture of the Mona Lisa and
     we ran away laughing through the galleries
I remember all that

I remember the after
The evening when I arrived late at the restaurant. I
        apologized and you said you forgave me.
During that meal you got up and went to the bathroom.
How embarrassed I was when you didn't return and I had
        to ask a women to see if you were in there.
You had gone home to teach me a lesson
Weeks later when your ex-boyfriend was in town you asked
        me to stay at my place because if I was there you said he
        wouldn't come to visit.
After you told me what a good time you had together and that he
        even fixed the leaking faucet that I had so long
        promised to repair.
That so swift end, those last weeks when your life became
        all investments and commodities.
If I wasn't interested, you said, that was just too bad.

I remember the day we parted. How you threw your arms around
        me crying, telling me you realized you were losing
        your best friend.
When I called about picking up the old laptop I had left behind,
        you told me you had thrown it out; and my bicycle
        locked up in the basement? You told me it had
        been stolen
We did not speak again.
Recently I opened that file folder, the one where
        we stored our travel photos
You must have gone through it before we parted tearing yourself
        out of them all.
I well remember our times together so long ago
I just can't clearly recall your face.

ICARUS IN THE BRONX

The Bronx
Home of brown brick in squat six stories, streets walled with
     parked cars.
Such a barren landscape, unloved, treeless, playground proof
Where terrors hung on the fists of toughs whose game,
     natural in his un-natural nature, was the big beating
     the small.
Poverty's children, hearts hardened by the prospect of growing
     up as janitors, laborers, marrying young, unhappy, joy
     only in drink, and bragging with the boys in the bar
Bitterness in the slur," Kikes own it, Micks run it, and
     Spics work it".
Sport, strength, daring, and speed the only valued virtues,
A stickball ace, bicycler with no hands, quickest at pinching
     candy from the corner grocery where one saw the
     fearful future,
The bent-backed owner hunched over sixteen hours a day,
     pinched faced, white haired, nickels and dimes, glaring at us

assumed thieves born of these brimstone streets.
Some, a Bronx bred few fed on a dream – escape.
But where, wasn't this the whole world, everywhere the same, where
      could one flee?
High up and away the most daring, far from those streets
      below, sought to fashion wings
Sneaking struts out of overcrowded classrooms, canvas woven from
      Public TV or borrowed books some with dreams for bindings.
Labored, hidden away from ridicule or worse, until that day,
      when to the street sounds of sirens and car alarms, on an
      updraft carrying the smell of overflowing garbage pails
They strapped on those wings and a few, a few did fly and fled that
      no-exit labyrinth below and found that this Bronx was not the
      whole world.

GREAT NEW YORK CITY ART SCHOOL STUDENTS

Life among us great artists
Noisy, loud, constant chatter – always arguing
When each of us knew everything, except when to shut up
But why, when we were all going to be tomorrow's great
       painters, poets, photographers, philosophers, politicians,
       great in all things that seemed to start with P
Hanging out together in a Lower Manhattan "P" for pad
The name for a student slum apartment in the East Village
Cold in winter, hot in summer, but cheap, with windows that
       leaked, ragged rugged floors, mattresses thrown
       about as if we were all camping in the wild
And girls, lots of girls, wild girls, all wanting sex,
       nothing but sex so they said in the stories
       we read about the lives of great artists
We nodded, how true, how true, as if we really knew.

Yet happy we were and forever would be, knowing exactly the
current artists to love and those to hate
Along with our greedy landlord, that nasty cop, guys who went
to work in suits, our last artistic creation which we never
quite finished but especially it was Mike who seemed so
out of place in believing he could hang out with us
great artists.
That life could not last forever
True, we all did become great painters, poets, photographers,
philosophers, politicians, things that started with P but
only in a past fondly remembered someday.
Meanwhile it would be P for partner (so, maybe she wasn't a
beautiful artist's model), parenting (paying for the new
winter coats and braces), a weekly paycheck
(earned 9 to 5 in a suit).
Not so long ago I met Mike by chance and we spoke about those
past good old days and he seemed like a really nice guy.

NEW YORK SUBWAY SINGER

Rush hour, jammed tight,
Around me blank faces, impatient, awaiting only their destination.
Above the subway's roar there came a voice, a rich baritone voice,
      singing.
No casual singer, a voice as one might hear on the operatic stage,
So beautiful, so powerful, clear even above the grinding of wheels
      on tracks.
I tried to turn to see the singer but packed shoulder to shoulder
      it was impossible.
The song from one end of the car was moving in my direction
      through the crowd.
Now, just behind me, from behind the solid wall at my back,
      it was an Italian aria.
A great cry of passionate love that one knew must surely end
      in tears.
I waited for a hand with a begging-bowl to appear through that wall
I might then be able to turn, perhaps able to put a face to this voice

But no, just an undulating wave as the voice passed by and on
  down the car
"Chi son?" (who am I?) the voice sang as if in reply to my curiosity.
"Sono un poeta. Che cosa faccio?"(I am a poet, and what do I do?)
  it sang while moving away from me.
Would I know more before it reached the end of the car?
"Scrivo" (I write). I recognized it. It was an aria from La Boheme
"E como vivo? (and how do I live?) I wanted to know.
Was he a professional singer, a subway beggar with a magical voice,
  or only a voice that I alone among these backs and shoulders
  unconcerned and unmoved could hear?
The voice rose to a crescendo, "Vivo" (I live!)
At that moment the doors opened. I raised myself on tiptoes to look,
  straining, but if he were there he was lost in the rush of people
  pushing to get out or in.
"Wasn't that wonderful?" I said to the man standing next to me.
He looked at me as if I were crazy.

ON THE SELLING
OF A PAINTING FOR
MILLIONS OF DOLLARS

What is it that makes this painting worth millions of dollars?
The beauty of its line, its vivid colors, shapes and forms,
      an emotion found there that causes the heart to
      beat the faster? One would like to think so.
Perhaps, a beat or two as well in contemplating the irony of how
      such a small fraction of that sum could have changed
      the artist's life.

Think! Modigliani dying of TB in his cold studio, Van Gogh's fatal
      guilt having to live off his brother, and those so many others
And "he" or she – we'll call him, "he"– what you have not heard
      his name?
Sadly "he" died alone in his studio among his sketches before
      he could complete the painting that might have sold for
      millions of dollars.
How costly it is to produce art, how expensive the primed canvas,
      stretcher bars, tubes of paint, brushes, studio rent
Always serious sums, but more so when the choice is between
      art supplies and hunger
With always the painful artistic questions, is what I am doing good?
      Is the dedication worth the sacrifice? Is it destined to be
      unseen, justifiably unknown and unloved, forgotten,
      or someday perhaps to be considered a masterpiece?

So what is it that makes a painting worth millions of dollars?
First, the artist must survive to paint it. Then most often it is not
the beauty of its line, the color, or that which makes the
heart to beat faster. One can't really put a price on that.
A million dollars is an economic value not an artistic one, the sum
of its appreciation as a commodity, an investment.

What might he have painted, if only he had had access to a bit
of that sum.
It might well have allowed that "he" to paint for us a great work
of art that makes hearts to beat the faster
Sadly "he" died.

YOU JUST DON'T CARE

You don't care that I care what you say or do
You don't care that I care finding your feelings so few
You don't care that I care that suddenly I knew
You don't care that I care that our romance is now through
      You just don't care

You don't care that I care for you haven't a clue
You don't care that I care that from my point of view
You don't care that I care that this conclusion I drew
You don't care that I care that I still care for you
      You just don't care

A BOARDING MANIFEST

They who refused to go
They, the rebellious ones
They had not heard of an ark
They did not believe the world was evil
That the murdering of millions was the answer
And who was this god who would end their world?
Not their god
Not made in their image
No, they refused to go.

They the "Plebeian Penguins"
No fancy dress for them, not as bankers in a
       boardroom prim and proper
Too casual for a want more world
Thinking what they wished
Coolly logical on rocky shores or ice
       covered cliffs
Creating vast oceanic concepts, a richer food

for thought than cooked canned cod
No, they too refused to go.

The "Feral Sheep"
No followers of the flock, cringing before
        the dog and the crook
To them the hills were too wide and too
        green to be told where to go
They wandered where their fancy took them
Noting the beauty of the view
Noting that freedom was more nourishing then
        trough tossed straw
No, they too refused to go.

The "Wooly Mastodon"
They were too few in number to go
Too few with furry flanks and long
        ivory tusks
They were family, they knew one another.
Who would leave a mother, father, sister,
        brother
To leave behind those one loves for a sea
        journey to a land of strangers?
If we all cannot go then we all shall stay
No, they too refused to go.

The "Simple Dodo"
Why should they go, why leave a world of
        such abundance,
A world that provides everything?
No need of wings for flight, or swift of foot on land,
Devoid of predators, no fear of death by claw
        or fang
Land of sweet scented breezes, sun and sea

This was paradise and who would leave such
        a world?
No, they too refused to go.

The "Homo Erectus"
They the upright and upstanding
Free of superstition and the desire for material
        possessions
Living in communities, in harmony with nature,
        where brother does not kill brother
Warmed by the discovery of fire, the cave painting,
        and the song,
Ignorant of talking snakes or sin, not fearful of
        thunder or threatening gods
Was not such a world right for them?
So they too refused to go.